AF270676

CHRISTOPHER COLUMBUS

Across the Ocean Sea

HEROES OF HISTORY

CHRISTOPHER COLUMBUS

Across the Ocean Sea

JANET & GEOFF BENGE

Emerald
Books

P.O. BOX 635, LYNNWOOD, WA 98046

Emerald Books are distributed through YWAM Publishing. For a full list of titles, including other great biographies, visit our website at www.emeraldbooks.com.

Christopher Columbus: Across the Ocean Sea

Published by Emerald Books
P.O. Box 635
Lynnwood, Washington 98046

Third printing 2021

Library of Congress Cataloging-in-Publication Data

Benge, Janet, 1958–
  Christopher Columbus : across the ocean sea / Janet and Geoff Benge.
    p. cm. — (Heroes of history)
  ISBN 1-932096-23-X
  1. Columbus, Christopher—Juvenile literature. 2. Explorers—America—Biography—Juvenile literature. 3. Explorers—Spain—Biography—Juvenile literature. 4. America—Discovery and exploration—Spanish—Juvenile literature. I. Benge, Geoff, 1954– II. Title.
  E111.B476 2005
  970.01'5'092—dc22

                                          2005001890

ISBN 978-1-932096-23-1 (paperback)
ISBN 978-1-62486-008-9 (e-book)

Printed in the United States of America

HEROES OF HISTORY

Abraham Lincoln
Alan Shepard
Ben Carson
Benjamin Franklin
Benjamin Rush
Billy Graham
Captain John Smith
Christopher Columbus
Clara Barton
Davy Crockett
Daniel Boone
Douglas MacArthur
Dwight Eisenhower
Elizabeth Fry
Ernest Shackleton

George Washington
George Washington Carver
Harriet Tubman
John Adams
Laura Ingalls Wilder
Louis Zamperini
Meriwether Lewis
Milton Hershey
Orville Wright
Ronald Reagan
Theodore Roosevelt
Thomas Edison
William Bradford
William Penn
William Wilberforce

Available in paperback, e-book, and audiobook formats.
Unit Study Curriculum Guides are available for many biographies.
www.emeraldbooks.com

Note to Readers

The voyages of Christopher Columbus were without question a turning point in the history of the world, and any study of history would be incomplete without delving into Columbus's fascinating and consequential life story. However, the inclusion of Columbus's story in the Heroes of History series is in no way an endorsement of all reported in *Christopher Columbus: Across the Ocean Sea.* Nor is it an endorsement of Columbus's apparent view of Christianity or of indigenous peoples. Our intention is to recognize Columbus's monumental achievements and far-reaching influence and to tell his story honestly in an effort to provide our readers with a panorama of American history.

The Heroes of History biographies are all written from the subject's point of view; therefore, this account of the life of Christopher Columbus reflects Columbus's viewpoint as much as possible, constraining the authors from commenting outright on events from other perspectives or detailing scholarly disputes. We encourage parents and teachers to discuss this book with young readers and assist them in exploring this important topic further. We encourage all readers whose interest is captured by *Christopher Columbus: Across the Ocean Sea* to consult varied sources and later historical perspectives to round out their understanding of Christopher Columbus, the Age of Exploration, and the lands and peoples encountered by and forever changed by Columbus's Enterprise of the Indies.

—The Publisher

Contents

Chapter 1

Marooned

Admiral, I don't think the *Bermuda* is going to make it," Bartolomeo Fieschi said as he stood beside Christopher Columbus on the deck of *La Capitana.*

Christopher, weak and feverish from malaria, stared across the ocean at the *Bermuda,* their sister ship. "Yes, she's in trouble, sinking lower into the water with each passing hour," he replied. "At this rate it won't be long before the waves start washing over her gunwales."

The first inclination Christopher had was to order the *Bermuda*'s crew to abandon ship, but to where? *La Capitana* was not in much better shape and could not handle the extra weight. "How are things below deck?" he asked.

"Our crew are slogging away, but the water just keeps pouring back in faster than they can bail it out. It won't be too much longer and we'll be sitting as low in the water as the *Bermuda*," Bartolomeo replied.

The two ships were making a desperate run for the island of Hispaniola, but it was now clear to Christopher that they were not going to make it. The head wind they were battling was just too strong, and Christopher knew he had to act fast to save the lives of his crew. He paced the deck, running his hand through his hair as he pondered his options.

"Come about to starboard," Christopher finally barked to *La Capitana*'s helmsman.

The helmsman acted decisively, pulling on the vessel's heavy tiller while sailors scurried above in the rigging, tightening lines and adjusting the sails for the wind change on their new heading.

La Capitana's bow slowly heaved to the right, each degree an effort with so much water in her bilges. The *Bermuda* soon matched *La Capitana*'s new direction. Meanwhile Bartolomeo raised his eyebrows and looked at Christopher. He did not have to speak; Christopher knew his question: Why south?

"I know Hispaniola is in sight, but with this head wind we'll never make it," Christopher explained. "If my reckoning is right, Jamesque is one hundred miles to our south. I explored there on an earlier voyage. The wind on this heading is more favorable, and we stand a better chance of making landfall before we sink."

"Let's hope your reckoning is right, Admiral," Bartolomeo said. "Everyone's life depends upon it."

"We'll make it," Christopher assured him.

Christopher then barked out another order for every available sheet of sail to be hoisted to take advantage of the prevailing wind. As the two ships plowed their way south, he kept a close eye on the *Bermuda*, half expecting her to sink below the water at any moment.

As the hours passed, Christopher scanned the horizon for any sign of Jamesque (Jamaica). He had seen nothing of the island when darkness finally descended and enveloped the two ships. On other nights the vessels would have lowered their sails and drifted together, not wanting to sail on and risk hitting a reef in the darkness. But things were too desperate now for such precautions, and Christopher ordered the ships ahead at full sail; he would take his chances. But an uneasy feeling crept over him as he stood alone on the poop deck of *La Capitana*. Would the *Bermuda* still be afloat in the morning? Or would she go to the bottom in the darkness, taking her crew with her?

As the first long, orange rays of sunshine streaked across the ocean surface the following morning, Christopher's fears were allayed. The *Bermuda* was still afloat—barely. And as the sun rose higher and began to sparkle on the bright blue ocean, Bartolomeo rushed to Christopher's side to point out an even better sight ahead. Emerging over the horizon was the lush, jungle-clad coastline of Jamesque.

"Your reckoning was right, Admiral," Bartolomeo said, relief evident in his voice.

Christopher smiled to himself. Whatever else he had been accused of in his life, being a poor navigator was not one of those things.

As Jamesque rose larger before them, Christopher recognized the lay of the land and gave the order for *La Capitana* to steer several degrees to port. The *Bermuda* followed their new course. An hour later the two ships sailed into a broad bay, Santa Gloria Bay, rimmed by a wide, glistening white-sand beach. Once again Christopher yelled out orders. "Dead ahead at full speed. Beach her as high as you can." It was an order he had never given before.

After the two ships were run aground, the men climbed off and ran around on the sand. They laughed and hugged each other. It was a satisfying moment for Christopher. Two crews had depended on him, and he had brought them to safety.

As he peered into the dense jungle beyond the beach, Christopher began to wonder what would happen to them next. It was true that they were now safe from sinking. But it was also true that they were marooned in an empty bay on an island an ocean away from home and not one person in the outside world knew where they were. Instinctively, Christopher called the men together for a Mass on the beach. Since his first memories as a small child, religious services had given him hope and inspiration, and he would need both if he was going to find a way to get himself and his men home again.

Chapter 2

A Boy from Genoa

Twelve-year-old Christopher Columbus* sat quietly in church. He listened intently as the priest completed the Latin Mass and began speaking in Christopher's native tongue—Genoese. It was July 25, 1464, and this was the sermon Christopher looked forward to most each year because it was about his namesake, Saint Christopher. He elbowed his little sister Bianchinetta so that she would listen too.

"The story of Saint Christopher, whose name means Christ bearer, is indeed one to which each

---

* In English-speaking countries, he is known as Christopher Columbus. He was christened Cristoforo Colombo, and Italians still refer to him by that name. The French call him Christophe Colomb, while in Portugal he was known as Christovão Colom. In Spain he was known as Cristóbal Colón.

person in Genoa can relate," the priest began. "Christopher, a giant of a man, lived in a small hut on the bank of a fast-flowing river. There was no bridge there for travelers to safely cross the river, so Christopher, using a large branch from a tree as his staff, would take a traveler upon his back and wade through the river to the other side, where he would gently lower the grateful traveler to the ground.

"One night as Christopher slept, a voice called to him. It was the voice of a child who asked for his help to cross the river. Christopher rose from his slumber and, taking the child upon his back, stepped into the river. But as he made his way across the river, the weight of the child became unbearable, and it took all of Christopher's strength to make it to the other side. As he put the child down, Christopher remarked that he would not have guessed that so small a child could weigh so much. 'Do not marvel, for in bearing me, you bore upon your back the weight of the whole world and Him who created it,' the child replied.

"Then, to prove his words, the child told Christopher to plant his staff in the ground near his hut and the next morning the staff would bear fruit. Christopher did as he was instructed. The following morning, when he emerged from his hut, where his staff had been there now stood a date palm blossoming in the early morning sunlight. And because of his faithfulness, we now venerate him as Saint Christopher, the Christ bearer, the patron saint of travelers."

As Christopher listened to the words of the priest, he imagined how one day he might travel away from Genoa and rely upon Saint Christopher for safety and good passage.

At the end of Mass, Christopher followed his parents, Domenico and Susanna, out of the cathedral. He paused for a moment to take in the panoramic view of the town and the harbor below. It was a scene he never tired of. White stone houses perched on the side of the Ligurian Apennines as the mountains gently swept down to the edge of the sheltered, deepwater harbor at the head of the Gulf of Genoa. The harbor was abuzz with ships from all over Europe. Some lay at anchor; others were tied up alongside docks that stretched into the harbor, unloading their cargoes or packing the finest products of Genoa into their holds. Still other ships were hoisting their sails and easing their way past the lighthouse that guarded the entrance to the harbor as they set out for exotic places Christopher had only heard about.

Since the ships came from and went to such far-flung ports, the streets of the city teemed with sailors and merchants from the Aegean islands, the Middle East, northern Europe, and North Africa. The entire town of Genoa was permeated with the smells and sounds of the sea, and gazing out over it, watching the ships come and go, seemed a fitting thing to do on Saint Christopher's Day.

Still, as Christopher watched his father greet several men from the Guild, he sighed. His was not to be a life at sea, or even around it. The life Christopher Columbus was about to embark upon dealt with wefts, worsted yarns, and carded wool. Now that Christopher was twelve, his father had announced that it was time for Christopher to follow in his father's and grandfather's footsteps and become a weaver.

Christopher could think of worse things to be, or at least he tried to. But even sheepherding or plowing would have taken him out into the open air he loved so much, whereas weaving meant sitting hour after hour at the loom set up in the front room of the family home. It was the same room in which they ate and entertained guests, the only other room in the house being for sleeping. It was the kind of confinement that Christopher did not look forward to, though he had some plans to try to make the job more bearable. When he got to be a little older, perhaps halfway through his apprenticeship in three years' time, when his younger brothers Bartholomew and Giacomo had joined him at the loom, he hoped to persuade his father to sell cloth farther down the coast of Italy. If his father agreed, Christopher hoped that he would be allowed to board one of the trading ships and take the cloth to market in person.

In the meantime, the years seemed to stretch out before Christopher like one of the spools of wool his mother spun. The only bright spot was the fact that his eleven-year-old brother, Bartholomew, would soon be joining him, and perhaps the two of them could have some lively discussions. Both boys had bright red hair, and their father often laughed that two redheads always made for a good debate.

When Bartholomew did finally come to work beside Christopher at the loom, the two brothers passed the time swapping imaginary tales of adventures far away from home and the ships that might take them to and from these adventures. But the truth was that very few of Christopher's relatives had ever been more than ten miles from Genoa, and Christopher's father did not like his son to go down to the harbor and talk to the sailors there. Too many of them were rough and dangerous people, he explained, sometimes kidnapping boys and tying them up until they were out of port, or even on occasion holding them for ransom until a family paid a high price for their return. Despite such warnings, Christopher and Bartholomew escaped to the harbor as often as they could.

As the years passed, Christopher was able to go out in small boats, fishing along the coast to the east and the west of Genoa, but he longed to go farther afield and see for himself some of the amazing things the sailors spoke about. His chance to do just that finally came when he was twenty years old. A wealthy Genoese family of shipbuilders sent him as their agent on a voyage to the island of Chios, located in the eastern Aegean Sea several miles off Asia Minor. The *Roxana*, the boat Christopher sailed in, was a large, three-masted vessel.

On the voyage out across the sparkling blue ocean, Christopher was particularly captivated by how the helmsman navigated and kept track of the ship's position by dead reckoning. He watched how the helmsman kept close watch of the direction of the compass, the speed at which the boat was traveling, and the direction and strength of the wind.

Using these pieces of information, the helmsman estimated the ship's position, which was then duly marked on a chart of the Aegean Sea. In this way the helmsman knew roughly how far the vessel had traveled and how much farther it had to go to reach its destination.

Sure enough, after the boat had been more than a week at sea, Chios emerged on the horizon. Christopher was impressed with the helmsman's skill. And he was impressed again when, using dead reckoning, the helmsman guided the voyagers safely back to Genoa.

Christopher was not the only member of the Columbus family infatuated with the sea. One day Bartholomew announced that he was moving to Lisbon, Portugal, to become a cartographer, or map-maker. This was an astonishing move, and Christopher wished his brother well as he set out to follow his new passion.

Bartholomew's decision unsettled Christopher, who began to search around for his own adventure. In August 1476, at the age of twenty-five, Christopher signed up as a seaman on a convoy of five ships carrying cargo bound for England and Flanders (Belgium).

As the Flemish ship *Bechalla* set sail and Genoa faded from view, Christopher felt the excitement pulse through him. This would be his greatest adventure, the farthest he had ever traveled from home. The *Bechalla* made its way in a southwesterly direction away from Genoa and sailed parallel to the French and Spanish coasts. Finally the limestone face of the Rock of Gibraltar at the southern tip of Spain slowly rose from the surrounding sea. It was an impressive sight, and Christopher stood on deck watching to starboard (right) as the ship slipped by the great rock and into the Straits of Gibraltar. Fourteen miles to port (left) lay the north coast of Africa. A short while later the convoy of ships had passed through the Straits of Gibraltar.

The Mediterranean Sea lay behind them now. For the first time in his life, Christopher Columbus was sailing on the Atlantic Ocean. The ships of the convoy set a northwesterly course as they sailed across the Gulf of Cádiz toward Cape St. Vincent, the most southwesterly point of Portugal. The captain had told Christopher that once they rounded the cape, they would head north up the coasts of Portugal, Spain, and France before sailing east into the English Channel.

All was going well with the voyage until the convoy rounded Cape St. Vincent. From behind the cape a fleet of thirteen pirate ships under the command of French buccaneer Guillaume de Casenove descended on them. The pirate ships opened fire on the five ships of the convoy, which in turn returned cannon fire. Back and forth the fighting raged for a good part of the day. Christopher watched as the captain of the *Bechalla* tried to use every breath of wind to his advantage, maneuvering his ship into the best position to get off damaging cannon shots at the pirate ships. When the cannons erupted and spewed their red-hot cannonballs toward the pirates, the *Bechalla* shuddered violently, and deafening noise reverberated across her deck.

Despite the valiant effort of the ships in the Genoese convoy, Christopher could see that it was hopeless. There were just too many pirate ships for them to overcome. But as the pirate ships began to move in to board and ransack the convoy, the men of Genoa were not about to give up. As the pirates approached, the Genoese sailors set barrels of pitch ablaze and catapulted them onto the pirate ships. Their plan worked perfectly, and soon four of the pirate ships were on fire. However, the Genoese ships were too close to the burning pirate ships, and soon three of them, including the *Bechalla*, also caught fire.

By the time the sun began to set, the four burning pirate ships had sunk to the bottom of the ocean. Despite their best efforts, Christopher and the other sailors aboard the *Bechalla* were unable to quell the flames on their own ship, which soon was completely engulfed and began to list to port. Christopher, who had been wounded in the fighting and had a bleeding, gaping gash across his back, knew it would be a matter of only a few more minutes before the *Bechalla* went to the bottom as well. He decided it was time to abandon ship. He leapt overboard into the cold water of the Atlantic and began to swim away from the ship. He soon found a spar from one of the sunken pirate ships bobbing on the surface of the water and grabbed onto it to keep himself afloat.

In the last, lingering rays of daylight, Christopher could make out the dark outline of the coast of Portugal at least six miles away, and he began to paddle toward it. His back throbbed with every movement.

Christopher spent a long, cold night in the ocean, holding the spar tightly with one hand and kicking with his feet and splashing with his free hand as he inched himself toward shore. Finally, shortly before dawn, a breaker picked him up and deposited him on the beach. Exhausted and semiconscious from the effort of getting to shore and from the loss of blood, Christopher lay on the beach as the tide went out around him.

Christopher could barely recall being lifted up by several fishermen, who carried him to their village, Lagos. Some women dressed his wound and nursed him back to strength. Christopher spent several weeks convalescing in Lagos. When the residents of the village learned that he had a brother in Lisbon, they supplied him with a donkey and sent him on his way north to the Portuguese capital.

As Christopher rode to Lisbon, he was excited about seeing Bartholomew again. Perhaps his brother would have some new maps showing exciting places to sail to. Christopher was already eager for his next adventure.

Chapter 3

A Passion for Sailing

It was a bright, summer day when Christopher Columbus finally arrived in Lisbon, Portugal. Christopher immediately felt at home amidst the bustle of the forty thousand people who lived there. An hour after arriving, he found his brother Bartholomew at a waterfront inn, deep in conversation with a sea captain. Christopher watched as the captain talked and Bartholomew jotted down notes on a chart of the ocean that was laid out between the two men. When Bartholomew finally noticed Christopher, he leapt to his feet and embraced his brother. Christopher quickly explained how he came to be in Lisbon, and Bartholomew invited him to sit down at the table with him. Bartholomew introduced Christopher to the captain. He explained that the captain had recently returned from a trip down the west coast of Africa and was helping him to update his navigational maps of the ocean with his most up-to-date observations.

As Bartholomew explained the maps, Christopher admired his brother's handiwork. The hand-drawn map on the table was a work of art. How much Bartholomew had learned in the three years since he had left the family weaving business in Genoa and moved to Lisbon! Bartholomew explained that, on the map, only those landmarks that were useful to sailors for navigational purposes were marked. A network of lines radiated out from a series of compass roses across the ocean. These lines were called rhumbs, Bartholomew explained, and a captain could estimate his position and course at sea by following the rhumb lines from one compass rose to the next. The captain added that these charts were very accurate for sailing by.

When the meeting was over, Bartholomew took Christopher on a grand tour of Lisbon. As they walked and talked, Christopher realized that Lisbon reminded him a little of Genoa, though it was far more cosmopolitan. Lisbon was located eight miles above the mouth of the Tagus River, at a point where the river broadened into a lake. Bartholomew explained that Lisbon consisted of three distinct areas: the lower town on the narrow strip of flat land between the river's edge and the hills; the upper town, which climbed the side of the hills to the northwest; and the Alfama, the old Arab section of the city established by the Moors after they invaded and took control of the Iberian peninsula in 711. This last section of the city clung to the hills to the northeast. Since Portugal was the most westerly country in Europe, its ports were all located on the Atlantic Ocean, and from them caravels set out to sail ever farther south down the west coast of Africa or to the islands of the Azores. In addition, ships from all over the known world sailed into Portuguese ports to trade. The chief of all the Portuguese ports was Lisbon. Christopher was fascinated to see Flemish, Norwegian, Danish, English, Genoese, Venetian, and Berber ships in the harbor.

Christopher knew that Portugal's importance as a seafaring nation was due mostly to the vision of Prince Henry the Navigator, the third son of King John I of Portugal and his English wife. Prince Henry had died in 1460, sixteen years before. Christopher would have loved to have glimpsed this most influential man in the history of oceangoing navigation. It was not that Prince Henry had been a brilliant seaman or chart maker but rather that he had the money and the imagination to bring together the top ship designers, navigators, mathematicians, cartographers, astronomers, and instrument makers from every part of Europe and even some from the Muslim world. *What a time that must have been,* Christopher thought to himself as he wandered along Lisbon's waterfront.

From 1418 on, Prince Henry had sponsored many voyages of exploration in the hope of finding a new route to the Indies. The Indies were the source of the most important commodity not grown in Europe—pepper, the spice that made rancid meat edible. Since the Mediterranean climate was so hot in summer, meat kept for only a day or so before it started to go bad. Even though pepper was extremely expensive, those who could afford it swore that it was worth every penny they paid just to spice up their rotting meat.

Almost all of the pepper that arrived in Europe came overland from Asia through the important city of Constantinople. But in 1453, two years after Christopher's birth, Constantinople, a Christian city, was overrun and captured by Muslim Ottoman Turks, who made it the capital of their expanding empire. The Ottomans began to clamp down on the flow of goods that moved through their newly acquired city on their way to Europe. As a result, European merchants were desperate to find another route to the East that avoided Constantinople and assured the flow of pepper and other spices and goods to Europe.

Under Prince Henry's sponsorship, the most skilled captains of the known world had discovered the Azores, Madeira, and the Cape Verde Islands, and in 1434 Captain Gil Eannes had rounded Cape Bojador on the western bulge of the continent of Africa. Before Captain Eannes succeeded in doing this, many sailors feared that it was impossible to sail to the equator and beyond because the water south of the equator was boiling and alive with sea monsters. But now, as he looked south, Christopher knew that Portuguese ships routinely plied the waters off the western coast of Africa, pushing ever farther south.

Some trading posts had been established along the African coast, though the trading was often done from ships that anchored off shore and beckoned the Africans to come out to them in their dhows. Many captains felt that this reduced the chance of catching malaria and other deadly diseases that could kill whole crews in a matter of days. As a result of this trade, a steady flow of elephant tusks, chests of gold dust, and slaves came north to Europe in exchange for red caps, small bells, Venetian beads, and horses. But the real prize would come if someone could sail around the southern tip of Africa, if in fact there was one, and carry on east to the Indies. However, no one had yet sailed far enough south to have seen the cape that would mark the bottom of Africa, and the oceans in the southern hemisphere were uncharted and thought to be fearsome.

All of this knowledge fueled Christopher's imagination, but it also frustrated him. Christopher would have loved to have been one of those learned men that Prince Henry the Navigator had gathered around him, but even if the prince were alive, there was no way Christopher would have been a part of that group. Christopher had to face the truth: he was illiterate. Despite the fact that the age of the printing press was now upon them and learned men were sharing all sorts of information and ideas through books, he could not read the books. Christopher determined to do something about the situation. He might be twenty-five years old, but it was not too late to improve himself. He was going to stay in Lisbon and teach himself to read and write.

Following through on his plan, Christopher rose each morning before the sun and said his prayers. Then he pulled out a grammar book and a pen and set about learning to read and write in Portuguese and Castilian. Castilian was important because it was spoken in neighboring Spain and by many of the educated people of Portugal. (Christopher did not learn to read and write Genoese, because it was a local dialect and not a written language.) It was tough going at first, but soon Christopher had grasped the fundamentals of reading, writing, and speaking both languages, even if he spoke them with a Genoese accent. Once he had grasped Portuguese and Castilian, Christopher embarked upon teaching himself Latin, the language many old and new books were published in.

While he was learning to read and write, Christopher took lessons from his younger brother in how to draw maps freehand and then how to chisel the image of the maps into woodcuts that could be used to print copies of them. It was painstaking work, but Christopher did not get bored, because it made him think of the unmapped reaches of the ocean and how to navigate well.

After he had learned to read, one of the first books Christopher read was an account of Marco Polo's voyage to Cathay (China) and back titled *The Book of Marco Polo*. Nearly two hundred years before, when he returned from Cathay, Marco Polo had been imprisoned in Genoa. Christopher recalled as a child seeing the old jail and wondered what it must have been like for Marco Polo, cooped up in it as he dictated his travel experiences to a fellow prisoner. From Marco Polo's account, Christopher learned that the Indies had three parts: India, Cathay, and Cipangu (Japan). He read and reread some of the passages from the account until he knew them by heart. These far-off places that Marco Polo spoke of came alive to him. *The Book of Marco Polo* told of rubies, pearls, and sapphires and of enormous gold and silver mines. The book explained how the people of Cathay spun silk from worms, and it talked of the various strange spices that grew in the Indies. From the book Christopher also learned that 1,378 islands lay off the coast of Cathay and that about fifteen hundred miles out in the ocean east of Cathay was the gilded, garden island of Cipangu. Christopher took notes on all that he had read and learned and found his mind often returning to the Indies as Marco Polo described them.

The following year, when Christopher had become a competent mapmaker, he and Bartholomew started their own mapmaking business. Although it did not make them as rich as they had hoped, it gave Christopher the opportunity to do the thing he loved best: go down to the docks in Lisbon and interview captains and crews as they returned from sailing distant waters. He also had the satisfaction of knowing that each new rocky outcrop or sandbar that he charted made sailing that bit safer for those who navigated by the charts he and Bartholomew had drawn.

Occasionally Christopher was offered the opportunity to set sail himself. On one occasion he was employed as a sailor by a Genoese trading company based in Lisbon that was sending a cargo of merchandise to be sold in England and Iceland. Christopher reveled in the trip, taking notes on the prevailing wind and the stars and trying to learn as much as he could from the captain about navigation. The ship traveled up the coast of Portugal, Spain, and France and then around the southwestern tip of England, and further up to the port of Bristol. From Bristol the ship headed north through the Irish Sea and then made a turn toward the northwest for Iceland. Iceland was located at the extreme edge of the known world, and it was unlike any other place Christopher had been. The island was craggy and volcanic, and in places steam vented up from the ground and hung in the air. The island also had extremely high tides, and Christopher was told that in winter the days were very short. It was a harsh environment, and even though it was late summer, the temperature was colder than Portugal in winter.

After unloading his cargo in Iceland, the ship's captain decided to sail north and explore for a while. Christopher and the rest of the crew set the sails and headed for the west coast of Iceland. When they reached it, they kept sailing north. It was the farthest north any of those aboard ship had ever been. The crew had no charts to guide them in these waters, only the captain's skill as a sailor and his knowledge of the stars.

The ship sailed about one hundred miles north of Iceland before the captain finally gave the order to come about and set a southerly course for Ireland, where they eventually docked in Galway for several days. While docked there Christopher heard the tale of St. Brendan, an Irish monk who had left Ireland in an open boat and sailed west to unknown places. It was said that St. Brendan came upon unknown islands and at one point landed on a whale, where he found a mermaid.

As the ship set sail from Galway, headed south for Lisbon, Christopher was delighted by all he had learned and seen on the voyage. His passion for sailing the ocean was rekindled during this trip, and he jumped at the next opportunity to go to sea. That came when another Genoese trading company employed him as their agent to go to Madeira and purchase a load of sugar.

Christopher eagerly set out for the island of Madeira, eleven hundred miles southwest of Lisbon. Madeira, the Azores, and the recently discovered Cape Verde Islands were the most westerly situated islands in the known world. As on his previous voyage, Christopher kept notes on the wind speed and direction and on important points by which to navigate. This enterprise proved to be the most profitable part of the journey for Christopher. When he reached Madeira, the sugar growers refused to extend credit to the Genoese trading company, and Christopher was forced to return home without the sugar.

By 1478 Christopher Columbus was an accepted and upstanding member of Portuguese society. He could read and write and had a solid mapmaking business and many friends. At age twenty-seven he decided he needed only one more thing—a wife. He set his sights on Doña Felipa Perestrello e Moniz, the twenty-five-year-old daughter of a noble Portuguese family. Doña Felipa's father, Bartholomew, who had died several years before, was a well-known navigator who had served under Prince Henry. As a reward for his efforts, Bartholomew Perestrello had been made lord of Porto Santo, one of the islands in the Madeira group.

Christopher and Doña Felipa were married in late summer and immediately set out with Felipa's mother to honeymoon at Porto Santo, where Felipa's brother was now the lord. When they arrived on the seven-mile-long, barren, treeless island twenty miles northeast of Madeira, Doña Felipa's mother gave Christopher several sea chests filled with her late husband's documents, navigational charts, and records. Christopher pored over them. As usual he studied the prevailing winds and made notes on the maps and charts to add to the notes Bartholomew Perestrello had already jotted down.

By the time of their first wedding anniversary, Christopher and Doña Felipa were still on the island of Porto Santo, and Felipa had given birth to a baby, a son they named Diego.

After staying nearly two years on Porto Santo, Christopher and Doña Felipa and baby Diego moved to Funchal on the island of Madeira. From there, in 1482, Christopher joined a royal convoy sailing to the Portuguese trading post at São Jorge da Mina on the Guinea coast of Africa. On this voyage, as on previous voyages, Christopher learned as much about sailing and navigation as he could. He practiced his dead-reckoning skills and the art of checking their accuracy by working out the ship's latitude from sighting the North Star. He also kept a close eye on the prevailing winds. On this voyage he noticed something interesting about the winds that he noted on his chart. The farther south they went, the stronger the winds blew from east to west. The trip also provided Christopher with a lot of practical information about the kinds of supplies needed for a long sea voyage and how the supplies were best stored on board ship. Christopher also noted the type of goods the natives on the coast of Africa liked to trade for.

By now Christopher had learned so much about sailing and navigation that, on a second voyage to the trading post at São Jorge da Mina, he was made a captain of one of the caravels in the convoy. It felt good to him to be master of his own vessel. He was impressed with how well the little caravel handled as she plowed forward down the coast of Africa.

By the time he was thirty-two, Christopher could look back on a life well lived. He had started out the illiterate son of a Genoese wool weaver and was now a respected member of the Portuguese upper class, a good reader in Portuguese, Spanish, and Latin, and a proud husband and father. In addition, he had sailed most of the coastline of the known world, from the Arctic Circle north of Iceland to the equator. All of these achievements should have made Christopher content, but they did not. Instead he longed for some new adventure, something almost beyond imagining—sailing *west* to the Indies.

At first Christopher told few people about his idea. Instead he kept a list of reasons why it should be possible to sail to the Indies, not by going around the bottom of Africa but by heading west across the Ocean Sea, as the Atlantic Ocean beyond the Azores was called. He read and reread his list every day, adding new information and points until he had listed the following six solid reasons why such a crazy venture could in fact succeed:

One. A captain had reported sighting a carved piece of wood drifting hundreds of miles west of Cape St. Vincent. He suggested that the carvings were from Cathay.

Two. On an island in the Azores, two dead bodies had floated ashore. According to eyewitnesses they were not Europeans; their skin was dark and their noses flat.

Three. Since the time of the ancient Greeks and Egyptians, educated people had believed that the earth was a sphere. The only problem was that no one was exactly sure how big that sphere was. The Greeks had even divided the sphere up into 360 degrees of longitude and latitude, but no one knew how big one of those degrees of longitude and latitude was. Christopher had set his mind to research the task. After reading the writings of many ancient scholars, among them those of the astronomer and geographer Ptolemy, he finally came to the conclusion that each degree of longitude was fifty-six miles, making the earth's circumference close to twenty thousand miles. Thus, if he were to sail west for the Indies, given the position of Portugal, he would not have to travel too far across the ocean to reach his destination.

Four. Christopher had recently read a new book on world geography titled *Description of the World*, or *Imago Mundi*, by Cardinal Pierre d'Ailly. In the margin of the book, Christopher noted, "The end of Spain and the beginning of India are not far distant but close, and it is evident that this sea is navigable in a few days with a fair wind."

Five. In a letter to Christopher, Florentine cosmographer Paolo dal Pozzo Toscanelli wrote, "I perceive your noble and grand desire to go to the places where the spices grow." He then went on to assure Christopher that the voyage was not only possible but also "honorable...and most glorious among all Christians."

Six. A verse from the Second Book of Esdras in the Apocrypha of the Catholic Bible declared, "Six parts hast thou dried up." Christopher took this to mean that six-sevenths of the earth's surface was land and only a seventh of it was covered in water.

By the time Christopher had compiled his list, he was beginning to think of this new adventure as a divine mission, ordained of God. As his name suggested, he would be going forth as the bearer of Christ's light to unknown lands. So with all of this firmly in his head, Christopher made himself a promise. He would devote the rest of his time and energy to seeking the western route across the Ocean Sea to the Indies. He even had a name for his new mission—the Enterprise of the Indies.

Chapter 4

Rejected and Dejected

It was early 1484, and Christopher Columbus was waiting for an audience with King John II, the twenty-eight-year-old nephew of Prince Henry the Navigator and now king of Portugal. He intended to lay out his plan to sail westward to the Indies for the king in the hope that Portugal would financially back the trip. As he stood waiting to be ushered into the king's presence, Christopher paced nervously, praying and reciting to himself several verses from the Old Testament that he knew by heart. "The isles saw it, and feared; the ends of the earth were afraid, drew near, and came" (Isaiah 41:5). "The isles that are in the sea shall be troubled at thy departure" (Ezekiel 26:18). "He shall have dominion also from sea to sea, and from the river unto the ends of the earth" (Psalm 72:8).

Christopher believed that these verses all pointed to God's wanting him to find a better way to the East and promising that he would have safe passage. In addition to having spiritual reasons, Christopher had personal reasons for wanting his plan to sail to the Indies to succeed. He intended to ask the king that he be well paid for his efforts. He wanted to receive a percentage of the riches he brought back from the Indies and to be appointed governor of whatever islands he discovered on the way there. These seemed reasonable requests to Christopher. After all, it was he who was risking his life to sail across the Ocean Sea.

Finally Christopher was summoned into the king's presence. King John sat on his throne on a low dais. He welcomed Christopher to the royal court and asked him to lay out his plan. Enthusiastically Christopher rolled out the charts and maps he had brought with him and began his presentation, referring to the maps and charts to reinforce his points. Despite his enthusiastic best efforts, he could not help but notice how bored the young king looked. How Christopher wished he were giving his presentation to the king's uncle. He was sure that Henry the Navigator would not have been bored; Henry had been much too interested in exploration for that. Not only did King John look bored, but also he kept interrupting Christopher with the same infuriating question: "Do you think we are close to finding and rounding the bottom of Africa?" Each time Christopher gave the same answer. He did not know for sure whether or when a Portuguese captain would discover the bottom of Africa. Besides, he pointed out, it did not really matter, for if he found an easier and quicker way to the Indies, discovering the bottom of Africa was moot.

"But Portugal has fifty years of seafaring knowledge invested in trying to go around Africa to the Indies," King John replied. "And I think we are close to achieving that goal. Nevertheless, your plan is intriguing. I will put your case before a panel of the most learned men in Lisbon and will inform you when I have made a decision." With that, Christopher was shown from the throne room.

This was not exactly the response Christopher had wanted, but he comforted himself with the knowledge that the king had not said no outright to his plan. Christopher was certain that once a panel of learned men studied his plans, they would recommend to the king that he back his proposal to sail west to the Indies.

In the days that followed, Christopher did all he could to keep up with the deliberations of the royal panel. The group was made up of several high churchmen and two Jewish physicians who had a deep understanding of cosmology and astronomy. Christopher was devastated in early January 1485, when he received word that the panel thought his plan ridiculous and impossible to carry out. Christopher learned that the panel members took exception to his estimate of the earth's being twenty thousand miles in circumference. They believed the earth was much bigger than that and that the three thousand miles Christopher estimated he would have to sail to reach the Indies was not realistic. They believed that to get to his destination he would have to sail at least twice that distance, and no ship afloat could carry enough supplies to make a journey of that distance and duration.

When he heard this, Christopher hardly knew which way to turn. He had been so sure that God wanted him to discover a shorter way to the Indies, and now he did not have the backing he needed to make that happen. Still, he wrote in his journal, "The Lord closed King John's eyes and ears, for I failed to make him understand what I was saying."

Not long after this crushing blow, Christopher was astonished to learn that King John had taken him more seriously than he first thought. Although the king had refused to back Christopher's plan, he had dispatched a caravel to follow the route Christopher proposed to get to the Indies. It was a secret mission, and to guide him, the captain of the vessel had been given the information and maps Christopher provided to the royal court. The caravel had set out boldly from the Cape Verde Islands off the coast of Africa but had limped back into port several weeks later. The captain declared that it was impossible to cross the Ocean Sea.

Christopher was furious that King John had double-crossed him, and he grew bitter and disenchanted with the king and the Portuguese court. As he wondered what he should do next, tragedy struck the Columbus household. After a short illness, Christopher's wife, Doña Felipa, died, leaving

Christopher with five-year-old Diego to take care of and no plans for the future.

Christopher soon decided that his wife's death was a sign from God, and quietly he began to make plans to leave Lisbon and settle in Spain. He hoped to get a better reception from the royal court there. However, in case King Ferdinand and Queen Isabella of Spain did not approve Christopher's original plan, Christopher and Bartholomew came up with an alternative plan. They decided to close their mapmaking business, and while Christopher went to Spain, Bartholomew would go to England and seek the patronage of King Henry VII for the voyage to the Indies. If that failed, Bartholomew would sail on to France to seek the help of King Charles VIII. Both Columbus brothers hoped that some European king would give them the ships and supplies they needed to finally sail west.

Christopher decided to settle in the city of Huelva, in the region of Andalusia in southwestern Spain, where the Tinto and Odiel rivers meet and flow together to form the Saltés River, which in turn flows into the Atlantic Ocean. As the small ship carrying Christopher and Diego sailed into the Saltés River in early summer 1485, Christopher's heart sank. The two small ports, Huelva and Palos, located close to each other, were nothing like Lisbon. No foreign ships were anchored in their harbors, only small coastal vessels and fishing boats. And compared to the brightly colored buildings of Lisbon, Huelva and Palos were drab, uninviting places. Still, as they sailed up the Saltés, Christopher saw something on a bluff above the river that did catch his interest. It was a Franciscan friary, home to members of the religious order founded by Saint Francis of Assisi in 1209. One of the sailors told Christopher that the friary was known as La Rábida.

The ship had docked in Palos, and with nowhere else to go, Christopher and Diego set out on the four-mile walk to the friary at La Rábida. Christopher's heart was heavy as he walked up the hillside. His wife was dead, he had his five-year-old son to take care of, and his mapmaking business was closed. His prospects looked grim, and he wondered whether he had given too much to pursue his burning passion to sail west to the Indies.

Christopher rapped on the heavy, wooden door of the friary. Several moments later the door swung open. Antonio de Marchena met Christopher and Diego at the door. He invited them in and offered them a bowl of soup and some bread. As they ate, Christopher fell into conversation with Antonio. As it turned out, Antonio was a well-read scholar whose knowledge, especially of astronomy and navigation, impressed Christopher.

Christopher and Diego spent the night at the friary, and the two men picked up their conversation again in the morning. Antonio de Marchena happened to be a friend of local count Medina Celi, an important shipowner in nearby Cádiz. The following day he introduced Christopher to Medina Celi, and the two men immediately liked each other.

Christopher described his plan to Medina to sail west to the Indies and asked Medina if he would be willing to supply three or four well-equipped caravels in which to undertake the voyage. Medina was excited by Christopher's plan and at first agreed to supply the ships. However, as Medina thought more about it, he realized that such an undertaking would need the permission of the king and queen.

Medina wrote to Queen Isabella, telling her of Christopher Columbus and his plan to sail west to the Indies. Soon a summons arrived for Christopher to appear at the royal court. Christopher was delighted with the summons and arranged for Diego to stay on with the friars at La Rábida to be educated, and then he set out for the royal court, which was presently in Córdoba.

In 711 the Muslim Moors of North Africa had overrun most of the Iberian Peninsula and for five centuries had ruled over the bottom two-thirds of the peninsula. The northern third of the peninsula, divided into small kingdoms, had remained predominantly Christian. However, as Muslim rule to the south began to weaken, the kingdoms in the north banded together and bit by bit started to push the Moors off the Iberian peninsula. After a battle on the plains of Tolosa in 1212, the Moorish rule had been confined to the small kingdom of Granada in southern Spain. The marriage of King Ferdinand of Aragon and Queen Isabella of Castile had united most of Spain, and now the king and queen were attempting to drive the remaining Moors from Granada. As a result, the royal court was in Córdoba overseeing the siege of Granada.

On May 1, 1486, Christopher was ushered in for a meeting with the king and queen. He immediately liked Queen Isabella, and he realized he could easily be looking at his own sister. The women were about the same age, both had blue eyes and auburn hair, and both were devout people of faith eager to win more converts for God and the Church.

The king and queen, draped in their royal robes and wearing crowns, sat side by side on thrones. It did not take long for Christopher to notice that King Ferdinand was not nearly as interested in his plan as Queen Isabella. In fact, on more than one occasion the king grew frustrated as Isabella asked Christopher question after question about the proposed trip. However, no decision as to whether the king and queen would fund and back the trip was forthcoming.

Time after time Christopher was summoned back to meet further with the king and queen and answer more questions. And when King Ferdinand finally seemed to lose interest in Christopher's Enterprise of the Indies, Christopher began meeting with just Queen Isabella. The queen was always interested in his plans, and especially in the idea that the money made from trading with the Indies could be used to fund another war that would free Jerusalem from the control of the Muslims and restore it as a Christian kingdom.

On this front Christopher pressed another point that he was sure would pique the queen's interest.

Legend had it that located somewhere in the Orient was a powerful Christian state under the rule of a monarch known as Prester John. Christopher explained that Prester John was rumored to be fabulously wealthy and had an enormous army. He told Queen Isabella that if he were to sail to the Indies, he could locate Prester John and forge an alliance with him whereby he could send his army to help drive the Muslims from the Holy Land. The queen admitted that she was intrigued by this notion, but still no decision was made, and Christopher began to grow frustrated.

It seemed to Christopher that despite Queen Isabella's great interest in his Enterprise of the Indies, she and King Ferdinand were preoccupied with driving the Moors from Spain, and not until they had won this fight would they finally make a decision to back the journey. They made a token gesture of referring the plan to a commission for further investigation, but based on his experience with the royal commission in Portugal, Christopher held out little hope that they would approve his plan.

After being in Córdoba for two years, on March 20, 1488, Christopher received a letter from King John II of Portugal, asking him to return to talk more about his trip. As he thought about it, however, Christopher was a little apprehensive about returning to Portugal. After all, he had left Portugal to seek the backing of King Ferdinand and Queen Isabella, King John's rivals, and also had left many debts unpaid in Lisbon. But when he received assurances from King John that there were no hard feelings on his part and that he would be given immunity from those seeking to collect their debts, Christopher set out for Portugal.

When he arrived in Lisbon, Christopher knew that his timing was awful. The city was abuzz with the news of the return of Bartholomew Diaz. Several months before, Diaz had set out with three caravels and sailed south down the west coast of Africa. He traveled farther south than any European had been before, losing sight of land for thirteen days. But when he did find the coast again, he kept pushing south until he discovered and then rounded the Cape of Storms, which protruded into a very rough stretch of water. He explored that cape and soon realized that he had reached the bottom of Africa. Around this southernmost tip of Africa lay the way to the Indies. King John was delighted when he heard of the discovery, and full of enthusiasm, he renamed the cape the Cape of Good Hope.

While this was a proud and triumphant achievement for Bartholomew Diaz and the Portuguese, it was a depressing moment for Christopher Columbus. Christopher doubted that King John would be interested in sponsoring his proposed trip west across the Ocean Sea now that an alternative route existed to get to the Indies via the Cape of Good Hope.

Christopher soon learned that he was right. King John planned to put all of his spare money into securing the route to the East around southern Africa. With no hope of receiving patronage for his trip from the Portuguese, Christopher decided to return to Spain and try yet again to win the confidence of King Ferdinand and Queen Isabella.

When he arrived in Córdoba, Christopher was glad to be back near a woman named Beatriz Enriquez de Harana. The two had met the year before and fallen in love. Because Beatriz came from a family of butchers, and much of Christopher's social status came from being the widower of Doña Felipa Perestrello e Moniz, Christopher and Beatriz had chosen to quietly become husband and wife through common law. And later in 1488, Beatriz gave birth to a son, whom she and Christopher named Ferdinand.

For the next several years, Christopher lived in Córdoba with Beatriz and Ferdinand, all the while trying to keep up the interest of the king and queen of Spain in his project. Despite his best efforts, they refused to back the Enterprise of the Indies. So Christopher was delighted when he learned that on January 2, 1492, Ferdinand and Isabella had finally won their struggle against the Moors, who were now fleeing from Granada. In the eyes of many Spaniards, it was a great day for the Pope and the Church, as well as for Ferdinand and Isabella. Now that the Muslims had been pushed from the Iberian Peninsula, the monarchs felt that Spain could once again reclaim its place as a truly Catholic country. In an effort to make Spain even more of what they felt was a "Christian" country, the king and queen decided to banish all Jews from their realm as well.

With his own dreams foremost in his mind, Christopher hoped that the king and queen would now focus their attention more diligently on his Enterprise of the Indies. When he was summoned once again to meet with King Ferdinand and Queen Isabella, he prayed that his six years of frustration in Spain were over. As before, he laid out the details of his proposed trip to the Indies and answered many questions. But this time Christopher asked for some things he had not requested of the king and queen before. He told their Highnesses that he wanted to be given the title admiral. He also wanted to be made governor and viceroy of any islands he discovered on his voyage west and to be promised that he and his heirs would receive a 10 percent cut on all trade with these islands.

Christopher was bitter and disillusioned when the king and queen turned him down. He had been certain of Queen Isabella's support, but in the end she had not backed him. Christopher wondered whether she had just been toying with him all these years, amusing herself by leading him to believe that he had her backing. Frustrated and angry, Christopher stormed out of the royal court.

Now that it was clear that Spain was not going to back the Enterprise of the Indies, Christopher decided to leave Spain and go in search of his brother Bartholomew. He had not heard from his brother since the two of them had parted ways in Lisbon six years before. Leaving his family to await his return, Christopher set off. He had nearly reached the port city of Cádiz when a royal messenger caught up with him. The king and queen had sent the messenger to urge Christopher to return to the royal court. Christopher wondered whether this would be just another of their games, but deep down inside he hoped that they had had a change of heart. His hopes, however, were dashed yet again. It was plain to him that Queen Isabella had changed her tune and was once again behind the voyage, but King Ferdinand refused to grant him the terms he asked. Once again Christopher left the Spanish royal court feeling crushed and dispirited.

Christopher set out again for Cádiz. This time he had walked only ten miles, to the bridge in the village of Pinos-Puente, when the same royal messenger caught up to him. The messenger begged Christopher to return to court with him. But Christopher had had enough; he was not going back to be insulted again. However, the messenger kept pleading for him to return, and eventually Christopher gave in. Questions kept flickering through his mind: What if the king had now changed his mind? What if Ferdinand and Isabella were both ready to support his venture? What if they were prepared to meet his demands? Christopher knew that he could not live with himself if he did not return with the messenger this one last time. Wearily he turned around and headed back to the royal court.

Chapter 5

Enterprise of the Indies

Once more Christopher Columbus entered the throne room and stood before King Ferdinand and Queen Isabella. After an exchange of pleasantries, they got down to business. Isabella explained that Luis de Santángel, the royal treasurer, had persuaded their Highnesses to change their minds. Luis de Santangel had pointed out all of the positive benefits Spain would reap if Christopher was successful in reaching the Indies. The queen also noted that with the Moors finally defeated, the royal treasury now had money to cover the cost of such a trip. The monarchs also reasoned that it was a good time for Spain to reach out with the light of Christ to the rest of the world. As a result, Isabella and Ferdinand had changed their minds and would now lend their support and patronage to Christopher's voyage west.

Christopher could scarcely believe what he was hearing. After so many years of trying to get royal support for his Enterprise of the Indies, he now had it, just like that. He wanted to let out a whoop of delight, but since he was in the royal throne room, he simply smiled gratefully.

Soon a document called the *Capitulations* was drawn up. It outlined the various points that the sovereigns and Christopher had agreed upon. The document acknowledged that Christopher Columbus had been engaged by Spain "to discover and acquire certain islands and mainlands in the Ocean Sea" and that Christopher would be awarded the titles of Admiral of the Ocean Sea and viceroy and governor over all the lands he discovered. In his role as admiral, Christopher would have power over all those who sailed in the waters he claimed for Spain. He would also have authority to settle any disputes that arose and to try cases of piracy, mutiny, treason, and other such acts. In his role of viceroy and governor, Christopher would have complete power over all the lands that he discovered and could appoint to and remove from office all officials in those lands. In addition, the *Capitulations* promised Christopher 10 percent of all gold, silver, gems, precious metals, and spices that came from the lands he discovered. On top of this, Christopher had the right to invest in one-eighth of any Spanish ship sent out to trade with the Indies. These rights, so outlined, would pass to Christopher's sons and their successors in perpetuity. In return Christopher would have to come up with one-sixth of the cost of the trip.

Following the signing of the *Capitulations*, Ferdinand and Isabella gave Christopher an official letter of introduction to the great khan of Cathay (China). Queen Isabella also ordered the town of Palos to provide Christopher with two ships for the journey as settlement for a fine that the town owed the royal court for smuggling goods into Spain from Africa.

The next week was a busy one for Christopher. It felt strange to finally be preparing for the voyage he had dreamed of for years. He held several meetings with the royal chancellor to work out the details of the royal involvement in his Enterprise of the Indies. Together they agreed that three representatives of the Crown should go along on the voyage with Christopher. The first was Rodrigo de Escobedo, who would serve as secretary of the fleet and make an official record of all discoveries. Then there was Rodrigo Sanchez, the royal comptroller, whose job it was to keep track of all gold, jewels, and other precious cargo brought aboard the ships, to make sure that nine-tenths of it was handed over to the king and queen upon their return from the East. The third man was Pedro Gutiérrez, the king's butler, who was given the duty of chief steward.

The chancellor also provided Christopher with a passport and a piece of paper that introduced him to all sovereigns he might encounter as "the noble gentleman Christopher Columbus, who is charged with certain duties and enterprises affecting the service of God and the increase of the Christian faith, as well as Our advantage and profit." The document, of course, was written in Spanish, though Christopher did find an Arabic speaker to sign on as the Enterprise of the Indies' official interpreter. He felt confident that whatever people they encountered in the Indies would be able to understand Arabic, since scholars agreed that Arabic was the original language of the world and that all other languages were based upon it.

Next Christopher prepared to leave Diego, now home from the Franciscan friary, and Ferdinand with Beatriz in Seville, along with some money to cover the family's costs while he was gone. Together the family went to Mass to pray that Christopher and his crews would have a safe passage across the Ocean Sea to the Indies.

With all these matters taken care of, Christopher made his way as fast he could to Palos. On his arrival there, he went straight to the waterfront, where five caravels lay at anchor. As he gazed at the ships, Christopher felt a surge of pride: the townspeople did not know it yet, but the king and queen had promised him two of those ships, and with God's help he would sail them west to the Indies.

Christopher's next stop was the friary at La Rábida. As he climbed the path that led to the friary, he thought about the first time he had visited. He had held five-year-old Diego's hand and urged him to keep walking. So much had changed in the six years since that day. Now he was no stranger showing up at the friary's door but an appointee of the king and queen of Spain, about to chart the boundaries of the Indies on the other side of the Ocean Sea.

When Christopher reached the friary, the Franciscan monks gave him a warm welcome. Christopher told them of his royal mission, and immediately they ordered a special Mass be said for him and promised to pray for him each day until he safely returned.

The following day Christopher visited Father Juan Pérez at the Church of Saint George in Palos, where a second Mass was said for him and his undertaking. After that, Father Pérez read the proclamation of Queen Isabella, requiring that the city of Palos supply Christopher with two ships within ten days' time.

Requisitioning the ships proved to be a simple task. The city council immediately ordered that two caravels, the *Niña* and the *Pinta*, be put under Christopher's command. On first inspection, Christopher was not particularly impressed with the choice of vessels. The *Niña* was about seventy feet long and twenty-one feet across the beam (width), with a draft of seven feet. She could fit about seventy tons of cargo into her hold. The *Pinta* was slightly larger. Both vessels had outboard rudders to steer them and high poop decks. They also had three short masts, though the *Pinta* was square-rigged, while the *Niña* was lanteen-rigged, with triangular sails like a Portuguese caravel. Both ships carried stone ballast. The two caravels were sound enough, but what concerned Christopher was that they were built for coastal trade and exploration and not for the long ocean voyage they were about to undertake.

Another ship was needed for the voyage, and Christopher chartered a ship from Galicia named the *Santa María*, which happened to be lying at anchor in the harbor at Palos. She was bigger than both the other ships and was square-rigged. Her main mast was higher than the vessel was long, with a yardarm as long as the keel. From the main mast hung a large, square sail, with a smaller, square sail mounted above. The foremast was about half the height of the mainmast and supported a square foresail. The shorter mizzenmast, set atop the high poop deck, supported a lanteen sail. The bowsprit swept up from the bow at a sharp angle and had a small, square sail mounted under it. Like the *Niña* and *Pinta*, the *Santa María* had an outboard rudder to steer her. The tiller that controlled the rudder was located one deck below on each of the ships. This meant that the helmsman could not see where the ship was headed and had to be directed by the captain from the deck above as to where to steer the ship.

Now that he had the ships for the journey, Christopher needed crews to man them. He chose Juan de la Cosa, the owner of the *Santa María*, to captain her. Martín Alonso Pinzón would command the *Pinta*, while his brother Vicente Yáñez Pinzón would captain the *Niña*. Christopher was not particularly pleased to have Martín Pinzón as a captain.

He found the man arrogant and hard to get along with, and the man seemed to take delight in pointing out Christopher's lack of sailing experience. Christopher knew that he had not been to sea in nine years, while Martín was a famous seafarer and came from one of the leading shipping families in Palos. Despite his dislike of Martín, Christopher had appointed him captain because he realized that his name and reputation would make it easier to recruit crews for the three ships.

Even with Martín Pinzón as captain of the *Pinta*, rounding up a full complement of sailors to man the three ships proved to be more difficult than Christopher imagined it would be. The officers for the voyage, including three other members of the Pinzón family and Beatriz's cousin Diego de Harana, signed up quickly. But regular seamen were more superstitious and much harder to persuade to sign on for a voyage to the end of the world. Queen Isabella had promised each sailor a generous sum of gold, to be paid in advance, if he signed on for the voyage, but even this did not prove enough incentive.

After two months of trying to recruit a crew, Christopher sent a letter to the queen, asking for her intervention. The queen replied with a royal decree stating that any convicted criminal who agreed to sail would have his sentence commuted upon his return. A day after she issued the decree, a full complement of crew, including twenty-four convicts, one of whom was a murderer, and three other men who had been convicted of trying to break him out of jail, had signed on for the voyage.

With a crew now recruited, the *Pinta* and the *Niña* were hauled out of the water at a local boat-yard, which happened to be a portion of beach set aside for the repair and refurbishing of boats. The two vessels were left high and dry on the beach by a neap tide, and work began on recorking their wooden planks below the waterline while they were repainted above it. At the same time that Christopher was overseeing this process, he was gathering supplies for the journey.

The ships were provisioned with salted fish, bacon, biscuits, flour, water, and olive oil. Christopher purchased new brass navigational aids: a compass, a quadrant, and an hourglass, which his cabin boy would have to turn repeatedly night and day so that Christopher would know what time of day it was.

On August 2, 1492, two and a half months behind schedule, Christopher finally felt that everything was ready for the voyage west. He gave the order for the crews to assemble aboard the three ships and promised that they would sail on the outgoing tide before dawn the following morning. Christopher watched as the ninety officers and crew boarded the ships. Apart from him, another man from Genoa, and a man each from Portugal and Venice, the crew were all Spaniards. Christopher noted that the reward of ten thousand maravedis per year that Queen Isabella had offered at the last moment to the first man to sight land on the other side of the world had finally gotten the crew excited about the voyage.

Before dawn on the morning of August 3, Christopher led the crew of the *Santa María*, the vessel aboard which he would be sailing, in prayer. Then he gave the order to cast off. Slowly the anchors on the three ships were hauled up, and the vessels drifted out into the river. Christopher smiled and let out a deep sigh of relief. His Enterprise of the Indies was finally under way. The ships were bedecked with the ensign of Queen Isabella flown from the foremast, and a flag bearing the lions of Castile and León flew from the mainmast of each ship, while a special banner for the expedition, a green cross on a white background, flew from the ships' mizzenmasts. As dawn broke across the Saltés River, Christopher relished the sight of the little fleet of ships under his command. He reasoned that if all went well, it would not be too long before the vessels were sailing into some port in the Indies.

As the *Santa María* sailed down the Saltés, it passed another ship, part of a fleet of vessels also leaving Spain that day. The day the expedition left was also the deadline for all the Jews whom Ferdinand and Isabella had expelled from Spain to leave. Any Jew who remained in Spain after August 3 was to be executed unless he or she embraced Christianity. As a result of the deadline, a flotilla of ships was leaving from ports along the southwestern coast of Spain. As the *Santa María* sailed past the vessel, Christopher looked across at the bedraggled Jews crammed aboard, clutching only those belongings they could carry in their arms.

Most of them, he knew, were headed for the Netherlands, the only country in Europe that had agreed to take the Jews in.

Christopher's own voyage, however, quickly recaptured his full attention. Once the *Pinta*, *Niña*, and *Santa María* had left the Saltés River behind, Christopher set a course for the Canary Islands, the last Spanish outpost in the known world. What lay beyond that was anybody's guess. But as he peered over the bow, feeling the salt spray on his face, Christopher was sure of one thing: his name meant Christ Bearer, and as such, he had been ordained to carry the light of Christ and the glory of the Catholic monarchs across the Ocean Sea to people who lived in darkness. As to the details of how this would happen, he had no idea. For now his attention was focused on navigating across the ocean to the Indies.

Chapter 6

Across the Ocean Sea

A fresh breeze sprang up as the three ships sailed in a southwesterly direction, their sails billowing in the wind. Within an hour of hoisting their sails, it was obvious to Christopher that the *Pinta* and the *Niña* were lighter, swifter ships, and they began to surge ahead of the *Santa María*, so much so that Christopher had the two vessels signaled to let out their sails so that they did not leave the *Santa María* completely behind. By nightfall Christopher estimated that they had traveled sixty miles.

Once he had calculated the day's distance, Christopher went to his cabin below the poop deck and cracked open the new journal he had brought aboard. He dipped his pen into the portable inkwell and wrote, "Friday, 3 August 1492. Set sail from the bar of Sáltes at eight o'clock, and proceeded with a strong breeze till sunset, sixty miles or fifteen leagues south, afterward southwest and south by west, which is the direction of the Canaries."

When he had finished writing, Christopher hurried back out onto the poop deck to lead the evening prayers, which he had already determined would include reciting the Our Father, the Hail Mary, and the Apostles' Creed and singing "Salve Regina," an ancient Benedictine chant.

With the last words of the Apostles' Creed recited, Christopher launched into "Salve Regina." The sailors and officers of the *Santa María* soon joined in. As he stood singing and watching the last remnants of dusk surrender the day to night, Christopher could hardly believe how the crew were torturing the sweet melody of the song! Most were singing off-key and at the same time were mangling the pronunciation of the Latin words. Christopher quietly prayed that either the crew would become more practiced at singing the chant or they would arrive in the Indies sooner rather than later.

It was completely dark by the time prayers and singing were over. The only things visible now were two small beacon fires, one on the *Pinta* and the other on the *Niña*. Christopher noted that the two fires seemed to have a calming effect on the crew, and he had to admit that they calmed him, too. As he watched the fires' glow, they reminded him that the *Santa María* was not alone. Two other vessels were with them, and together they would help each other across the uncharted water of the Ocean Sea.

The following day and the day after that things went well for the three ships, but on August 6 they encountered their first challenge. That day, referring to himself in the third person as the "Admiral," as he often did in his journal, Christopher wrote:

> Monday, 6 August. The rudder of the caravel *Pinta* became loose, being broken or unshipped. It was believed that this happened by the contrivance of Gomez Rascón and Christopher Quintero, who were on board the caravel, because they disliked the voyage. The Admiral says he had found them in an unfavorable disposition before setting out. He was in much anxiety at not being able to afford any assistance in this case, but says that it somewhat quieted his apprehensions to know that Martín Alonzo Pinzón, Captain of the *Pinta*, was a man of courage and capacity. Made a progress, day and night, of twenty-nine leagues.

By then the three ships were approaching the Canary Islands, but the wind suddenly dropped, and for the next two days the vessels floated helplessly. When the wind finally returned and the ships could sail again, Christopher ordered the *Pinta* to put in at Las Palmas on Grand Canary Island for repair to her sprung rudder. The *Niña* and *Santa María* sailed on to the island of Gomera, where men from the two ships went ashore to fill extra casks with water and to buy cheese and pickled local beef. Once these supplies had been loaded aboard, the ships sailed back to Las Palmas, where Christopher oversaw the repairs to the *Pinta*. New pintles, the iron pins on which the rudder pivoted, had to be cast in the only blacksmith shop in Las Palmas before the rudder could be reattached to the ship. Christopher hoped that no more metal fittings on any of the ships broke or were sabotaged. He doubted that they would find a blacksmith shop or boatyard in the Indies in which to make such repairs.

Repairs to the *Pinta* took much longer than Christopher had anticipated. However, he did not waste the time. He was not particularly happy with the lanteen rigging of the *Niña* and so decided to convert it to a square-rigger while they waited in the Canary Islands. Spars were added to the vessel's fore and main masts for extra support, and her lanteen, or triangular, sails were cut and sewn together to form square sails.

Finally, on September 2, the repairs to the *Pinta* were finished, and the three ships sailed back to Gomera, where they anchored off San Sebastián. On the way there they sailed past Tenerife, the largest island in the Canary group, where they were treated to the sight of El Teide, the island's 12,000-foot-high volcano, belching ash and lava into the air as it erupted. But while Christopher marveled at the sight, some of his crew took the sight of an erupting volcano as a bad omen.

Finally, after taking on still more supplies at Gomera, on Thursday, September 6, 1492, the

Pinta, Niña, and *Santa María* departed once again for the Indies. The ships headed west past the island of Ferro, but the winds were light. It took three days before the belching peak of El Teide finally sank below the horizon, and with it their last sighting of the Old World. All that lay ahead was new to Christopher and his crew, who were hopeful that they would soon touch the shores of Asia. But although Christopher was excited by this possibility, he noticed that many of the crew aboard the *Santa María* looked nervously westward. Christopher could understand their apprehension. He knew that many of the crew, some as young as twelve years of age, had never been to sea before. And of those who had, most had never sailed out of sight of land. Christopher reassured himself that they were only a week or two away from their destination, but in the meantime he decided to trick the crew into thinking that they were actually sailing fewer miles each day than they were. By his underestimating the distance covered, the crew would think they were not as far from home as they were. For now, Christopher decided not to tell a single person that he was keeping two sets of records. However, he recorded his plan in his private journal:

> Sailed this day nineteen leagues, and determined to count less than the true number, that the crew might not be dismayed if the voyage should prove long. In the night sailed one hundred and twenty miles, at the rate of ten miles an hour, which makes thirty

leagues. The sailors steered badly, causing the vessels to fall to leeward toward the northeast, for which the Admiral reprimanded them repeatedly.

Monday, 10 September. This day and night sailed sixty leagues, at the rate of ten miles an hour, which are two leagues and a half. Reckoned only forty-eight leagues, that the men might not be terrified if they should be long upon the voyage.

Tuesday, 11 September. Steered their course west and sailed above twenty leagues; saw a large fragment of the mast of a vessel, apparently of a hundred and twenty tons, but could not pick it up. In the night sailed about twenty leagues, and reckoned only sixteen, for the cause above stated.

Friday, 14 September. Steered this day and night west twenty leagues; reckoned somewhat less. The crew of the *Niña* stated that they had seen a grajao, and a tropic bird, or water-wagtail, which birds never go farther than twenty-five leagues from the land.

The course that Christopher had charted to take the ships to the Indies was due west from the Canary Islands. Christopher had determined that the Canary Islands at latitude 28 degrees north was the same latitude as Cipangu (Japan), and all he had to do was hold course and he would surely reach it. But Christopher had another reason for coming this far south before heading west. On his earlier journeys down the west coast of Africa with the Portuguese, he had noted the steady winds that blew west in these latitudes. Sure enough, three days after leaving the Canaries, he found the wind he was looking for. The sails on the three ships bellied, and soon they were headed west at a fair clip.

Life aboard ship fell into a monotonous routine. Every half hour, as the last grains of sand drained from the hourglass, a boy would flip it over. Eight turns of the hourglass was one watch. At first light, when the cabin boy turned the hourglass, he would sing:

Blessed be the light of day
And the Holy Cross, we say.

At sunset when he turned the glass, he would sing:

God give us a good night and good sailing;
May our ship make a good passage,
Sir Captain and Master and good company.

And when he turned the hourglass for the eighth time at the end of each watch, he would sing:

The watch is called,
The glass floweth.
We shall make a good voyage
If God willeth.

When the sailors were not on watch, they spent most of their time sleeping and fishing. Sleeping on a ship, though, was not always easy. Ships had no crew quarters. Only Christopher and the captain had cabins. When a sailor wanted to sleep, he had to find a space on deck and sleep there in his clothes. He did not even have to worry about taking his shoes off, since most sailors went barefoot.

One meal a day was served aboard ship at 11:00 AM. It was cooked over a bed of hot sand in a firebox on deck and consisted mostly of salt meat, dried peas, and hardtack, a hard biscuit made from flour and water.

Ten days after leaving the Canary Islands behind, Christopher wrote in his journal:

Sunday, 16 September. Sailed day and night, west thirty-nine leagues, and reckoned only thirty-six. Some clouds arose and it drizzled. The Admiral here says that from this time they experienced very pleasant weather, and that the mornings were most delightful, wanting nothing but the melody of the nightingales. He compares the weather to that of Andalusia in April.

The next day the three vessels sailed into an area of the Atlantic where the water was still and the surface was covered with brightly colored brown and yellow and green algae. Christopher and the crew thought that the area resembled a vast expanse of newly cut grass. It was, in fact, sargassum, and the sailors were all excited when they first encountered it. For them it could mean only one thing—land was nearby. But when no land was spotted, the sailors became glum and began to fret that the ships would get so tangled in the sargassum that they could not sail.

Christopher tried to encourage the men by pointing out that they were making steady progress through the sargassum and that the continent of Asia could not be far away. Sure enough, with favorable winds, the three ships plowed on. But the favorable winds themselves became a problem for the crew. The men became afraid that the prevailing easterly winds that were speeding them west would prevent them from ever returning in an easterly direction. They wondered how on earth they would ever be able to sail back to Spain against such wind.

Christopher tried to reassure the crew that they would make it home to Spain, that from his earlier sailing experience with the Portuguese he knew that farther north the winds changed direction and blew back across the Ocean Sea. However, the men were not convinced until they encountered a wind shift. The easterly winds suddenly died down, and the ships began to battle a head wind blowing from the west. Finally the crew's fears were silenced, and the men believed Christopher. With the change in the wind, the progress of the ships was slowed, and the three ships were able to maneuver close enough to each other so that their captains and Christopher could yell back and forth.

By now the men had begun to see pelicans, frigate birds, and other birds, and Christopher felt sure that they were approaching land. On one occasion a cry of "Land ho!" went up from a sailor on the *Pinta*. Christopher squinted toward the western horizon, where he saw what looked to be the vague outline of an island. Instinctively he sank to his knees on deck and thanked God for safe passage across the Ocean Sea. He then had the crew sing "Gloria in Excelsis Deo" before the ships altered course directly for the island. Alas, everyone's hopes were dashed when they realized that what they were headed for was just a cloudbank sitting low on the western horizon.

Christopher ordered the three ships to set course west once again. Dejected crew members did as he asked, trimming the sails while the helmsman pulled on the heavy tiller and brought the *Santa María* back onto a western heading.

Soon the ships emerged from the sea of sargassum they had been sailing through, right into another peril—a tropical storm. Rain pelted down, and the wind whipped the surface of the ocean into a frenzy. Swells taller than the ships soon confronted them, and the ships headed directly into the swells to avoid being swamped or capsized. Christopher was grateful for how well the three vessels handled the heavy sea as they rode up the face of the swell and then slid down into a trough before riding up the face of the next wave. Eventually the wind dropped, the ocean calmed, and the sun came out. Once again the ships headed west.

Despite the constant presence of pelicans, herons, albatross, sea swallows, and petrels—all birds that meant land must be somewhere not far away—by October no land had appeared on the horizon. Each day the crew grew more anxious. Supplies were running low, and Christopher was aware that some of the men were even talking about staging a mutiny and turning the ships around and sailing home.

Christopher tried his best to keep the men's spirits up. He told the men that he was certain they were on the right course for the Indies, that they had come this far and could not give up now. They were going to stay their course until they hit land. "If we do not find land," he told the crew, "you can cut off my head; that way you can sail home in peace."

On hearing this, Martín Alonzo Pinzón yelled back from the deck of the *Pinta* for the crews on the three ships to hear, "Adelante! Adelante! [Onward! Onward!] We have just barely left, and you're already thinking of turning back?"

Sail on they did. But much to everyone's chagrin, they continued to encounter flocks of birds but no land. Finally, on October 9, Christopher called a meeting of the three captains aboard the *Santa María*. He explained that he believed that the Indies were close at hand, but the near mutinous situation of the crew was of great concern. He told the captains that if they had not sighted land in three days, they would turn around and set sail back to Spain.

By October 11 the time for sighting land was running out. Even though it was late at night, the three ships sailed ahead through the darkness as fast as they could go. Christopher stood on the deck of the *Santa María* as she gently rocked back and forth, her sails bellying above him in the stout breeze. As he stared out into the darkness, he spotted a flickering glow of light on the far horizon, like the light from a little candle, rising and falling.

The ships sailed on as the moon rose in the night sky. Christopher had promised his crew that if land were not sighted within twenty-four hours, they would turn around and head for home. At two o'clock in the morning on October 12, the cry of "Tierra! Tierra! [Land! Land!]" went up from Rodrigo de Triana, the lookout on the *Pinta*. Christopher raced to the side of the *Santa María* and peered out into the darkness. Sure enough, there before them a white cliff shone in the moonlight. They had reached the Indies! At first light Christopher would go ashore and claim the land for Spain.

Chapter 7

San Salvador

Throughout the night Christopher watched with delight as the moon reflected off the cliffs of the land ahead. He had persevered and made it to the Indies!

At daybreak Christopher ordered the sails hoisted, and the ships rounded the southern point of what the men soon realized was an island. The men looked for an opening through the coral reef that surrounded the island. As he took depth readings with a lead-weighted rope, Christopher thought about what he should call this most important landfall. Should it be Isabella or Ferdinand after the king or queen of Spain, or Española after Spain itself? Then an idea came to him. It was God who had provided safe passage this far and preserved the lives of Christopher and his crew in the midst of great danger, and it was He who should be honored first. Christopher felt sure that the king and queen would approve as he whispered the name *San Salvador*—Holy Savior—to himself.

An entrance through the reef was soon found, and the *Pinta, Niña,* and *Santa María* all sailed into safe harbor on San Salvador's eastern side. The crew laughed and sang for joy as they dropped anchor; they were not doomed to die on the Ocean Sea, as many of them had come to believe.

Meanwhile Christopher was below deck supervising his cabin boy as he pulled out a flag wrapped in oilskin and brought it up on deck. Christopher heaved a sigh of relief as the royal standard of Spain was unfurled. The flag was still in the same pristine condition as it had been when he last checked it upon leaving the Canary Islands thirty-five days before.

Within minutes Christopher was climbing down a rope ladder over the side of the *Santa María* and into a longboat to be rowed ashore. Along with several sailors who would row the boat, seated in the longboat were Rodrigo de Escobedo, secretary of the fleet and notary, who would officially record the flag-planting ceremony for their royal Catholic Highnesses in Spain, and the Arabic interpreter, Luis de Torres. The cabin boy dutifully climbed down the ladder next, and then the flag was handed over the railing to him. Once everyone was aboard, the longboat was rowed toward the white sand beach, followed by Martín Alonso and Vicente Yañez Pinzón in their own longboats. The Pinzóns stayed a respectful distance behind, allowing Christopher's boat to be the first to scrape the sandy shore. When it did, Christopher stood up and stepped into the water, unaware that he was now standing in the Western Hemisphere. He waded ashore, fell to his knees, and thanked God for bringing him and his crews safely to San Salvador. Tears spilled down his cheeks as the momentous achievement of finding the Indies overcame him.

By now the Pinzón brothers and members of their crews were also on the beach. Christopher motioned for the cabin boy to bring him the flag. With a prayer on his lips, he sank the flagstaff into the sand. Then he stood back and declared, "I Christopher Columbus, now Vice-Regent and Governor-General, Lord Admiral of the Ocean Sea, in the name of the King and Queen of Spain, do take formal possession of this domain, which will forthwith be named San Salvador."

All the Europeans on the beach—about twenty of them—cheered and shouted, but Christopher soon became aware of other eyes watching. Through the tangled trees he could make out the shapes of naked men staring at them. For a moment Christopher thought about the wonderful day this was for these men. Today was the first day in all history that they would come in contact with the good news of salvation, and if God willed, today might even be the day some of them would embrace the Christian religion.

As the cheering died down, two native men emerged from the shadows and advanced slowly toward the crew. This gave everyone ample time to study one another. Christopher was astonished to find that these men did not look at all like any man from Cathay (China) that he had heard described. The men were short, with copper-colored skin, wide foreheads, and large, round eyes. Their hair was short and coarse like that of a horse's tail, and it was combed toward their foreheads, except for a small portion at the back that hung down their backs. The two men were also naked, and one of them had smears of red and black paint or dye across his face, chest, arms, and legs. Christopher was unsure what to make of the men as they approached. His spirits rose when he noticed that they both appeared well fed. He decided that the island must afford them a good supply of food.

One of the natives—or Indians as they were soon being called—walked right up to Christopher. He stared intently at his sword, which Christopher gingerly pulled from its scabbard. Christopher held out the sword to the native, who reached for it and grabbed it by the blade, cutting his hand. Christopher realized that the men had probably never seen iron or steel before and that it was the sword's shininess that had attracted their interest.

Soon other native men who had been watching from the bushes emerged onto the beach. Most of them seemed young; Christopher guessed that the oldest man was thirty at the most. He also noticed that a number of the men had scars on their bodies, and using signs and gestures, he asked them how they got the scars. Replying in the same manner, the men indicated that they had received the scars defending themselves against people from another island nearby who had attacked them. Christopher immediately thought that these others could only be men from the continent of Asia. He let out a sigh of relief; the continent he had expected to find was not far away. Maybe in a few days they would make it there.

The native men talked among themselves in a language unlike any Christopher had ever heard before. Christopher motioned for Luis de Torres, the expedition's interpreter, to step forward. Luis was fluent in Arabic, considered the root of all languages, and Christopher knew that if anybody could make sense of these men's language and communicate with them it would be he. Luis began talking to the natives of the island in slow, simple Arabic. But the natives did not appear to understand a word he said. Christopher was shocked, and for a brief moment he wondered whether he had made other wrong assumptions as well. Finally, feeling that everything ashore had gone well, Christopher decided it was time to head back to the ships.

No sooner had he reached the *Santa María* and climbed aboard than Christopher noticed that the natives from the island were swimming out to the ships. Soon native men, women, and children were clambering aboard the three vessels. Like the men on the beach, they were all naked, and they carried with them parrots, balls of cotton thread, javelins, and other items that they gladly exchanged with the Spaniards for glass beads, hawk's bells, and other small items. Christopher ordered that the natives be treated with respect by the crew, and by the time the natives had left and had swum back to shore, he was certain that good will had been built between his crew and the natives. It had been a great and successful day.

After the natives left, Christopher began writing a report to the king and queen detailing the day's events:

> As I saw that they were very friendly towards us, and decided that they could be much more easily converted to our holy faith by gentle means than by force, I presented them with red caps and strings of bead necklaces, and many other trifles of small value, with which they were much delighted, and became amazingly attached to us.... It appears to me that the people are ingenious and would be good servants and I am of opinion that they would very readily become Christians, as they appear to have no religion. They quickly learned such words as are spoken to them. If it please our Lord, I intend to carry home six of them to Your Highnesses, that they may learn our language...unless Your Highnesses should choose to have all of the islanders transported to Castile, or held captive in the island. I could conquer them all with fifty men, and govern them in any way I pleased.

Christopher spent the rest of the day aboard the *Santa María*. He often looked toward San Salvador and smiled at the sight of the royal standard of Spain waving in the breeze on the beach. The Indians had not touched it, which he took to be a sign of their continued welcome. That night Christopher took an extra long time saying his prayers, as he had so much to be grateful for: the welcoming natives, the possibility of fresh water and food, and the knowledge that he would be hailed as a hero when he returned to Spain.

As he lay in bed that night, Christopher thought about how surprised and shocked he was that the natives were naked and did not speak Arabic. How could they be from the Indies? Then he came up with an answer. He conjectured that although he was in the Indies, he was on one of the outer islands that dotted the coast of Cathay—an island that the people of Cathay did not even know about. Somewhere out there was the mainland of Cathay and the island of Cipangu (Japan), and he would keep sailing until he found them.

The following morning Christopher was awakened at dawn by a bumping sound, followed by several yells from the morning watch. He got up to see what the problem was. His heart raced as he walked out onto the poop deck, where he discovered that the commotion was being created by a fleet of strange-looking native boats swarming the three ships at anchor. These native boats were unlike anything Christopher had seen before. They were made from single tree trunks, and some of them were big enough to hold twenty or more men, while others held only a single man. The boats were swift in the water and were rowed using an oar shaped like a baker's peel. If for some reason one of the boats capsized, all the men aboard would jump into the sea and swim until they had righted the boat and bailed it out.

Like the natives the day before, the men in the strange boats came loaded with balls of cotton, parrots, javelins, and other items that they wanted to exchange for whatever the Spaniards would give them.

As the native men came aboard to trade, Christopher noticed that a number of them were wearing gold jewelry. Some hung the jewelry around their necks like a pendant, while others wore it hanging from pierced holes in their noses. Once again using gestures and signs, Christopher inquired where the men had gotten the gold. The men signaled back that it had come from a king who possessed large numbers of vessels made from gold. But when Christopher inquired as to where this king was, the response of the native men was confusing. Some men pointed in the direction of the far side of the island, while other men pointed south. When Christopher pressed them further about the location of the king and his gold, the men finally admitted that they did not know exactly where the king was. However, they did assure Christopher that there was more land to the south of the islands, as well as to the southwest and northwest. There, they told him, he might find the king with the gold vessels.

Christopher decided to stay and explore San Salvador island until the following evening, when he would head south in search of the source of the gold. After the native men left the ship, Christopher and several crew members went ashore to explore the island. They discovered that San Salvador was about thirteen miles long and six miles wide and in the middle had a large lake, out of which flowed a number of small streams. The whole island was covered with lush trees and foliage. It was very different from the Canary Islands they had left behind on the other side of the Ocean Sea.

The next morning, soon after the sun rose across the sparkling, clear water of the lagoon where the ships were anchored, Christopher once again climbed over the side of the *Santa María* and into the longboat. Before he set out, he ordered the men to empty the remaining water jars aboard the ships and refill them all with fresh water from the streams on the island. Then it was time to circumnavigate the island in the longboat. The sailors' brawny shoulders tugged at the oars, and the boat was off.

Since the ships were anchored at the eastern end of San Salvador, the longboat headed north around the top of the island. Soon after rounding the northern tip of the island, the men encountered a village. The residents of the village raced to the water's edge and called out to Christopher and his men in the boat. Christopher, however, decided not to stop at the village. A lot of jagged rocks were near the shore, and Christopher did not want to risk punching a hole in the longboat on one of them. But if he would not stop, he soon learned that the natives were determined to come to him. They plunged into the water and began swimming out to the boat. They clung to the gunwales and stared at the Spaniards. Then some of the bravest ones reached out to touch the white men's arms and faces. As with the people on the eastern end of the island, they were soon trying to communicate with Christopher through hand signs and gestures. They seemed to want to know if their visitors had come down from heaven.

Once friendly relations had been established, more natives swam out to the boat, bringing with them food and fresh water to drink. Christopher and the sailors hardly recognized any of the foods: a fruit covered in sharp prickles that tasted something like an apple, and cooked cassava root, which had a fibrous texture and a bland taste. At first the men were reluctant to eat the food, but for the sake of building rapport with the natives, Christopher led by example.

After they had eaten some of the food, the men waved good-bye to the natives and rowed on. They encountered two more villages along the coast of the island, and at each one they had a reception similar to the one at the first village.

Finally, at midafternoon the longboat arrived back at the *Santa María*. The water jars had been refilled with fresh water as ordered. The captains had also traded lace points, tiny metal cones that were used on lacy collars back in Europe, with the natives for a supply of local food. The men in the longboat groaned when they saw piles of cassava roots being loaded into the hold. Christopher smiled to himself. He reasoned that bland food was better than no food at all and that when the men got hungry enough, they would gladly sit down to a meal of cooked cassava root.

Late in the afternoon, as the sun began to sink toward the horizon, it was time to leave San Salvador. Christopher had several of the crew row ashore and retrieve the royal standard he had hoisted on the beach. He hoped to find many more shorelines on which to place the flag and claim the land in the name of Spain. He also had his crew capture the last seven Indian men who came aboard the *Santa María*, hoping that they would make good guides to the gold-laden lands that surely lay to the south and west. When one of these men dived overboard, swam ashore, and escaped, the remaining six were taken below deck and chained up. Christopher then ordered anchors aweigh and the sails hoisted. The *Pinta*, *Niña*, and *Santa María* slipped out through the gap in the reef and were soon off, running before the wind to the next stage of their grand enterprise.

Chapter 8

Still More Islands

The ships sailed southwest, and late the next afternoon another island floated across the horizon. The name Santa María de la Concepción came to Christopher's mind, and he decided that it was the perfect name for this second island he had discovered. The Virgin Mary had, he believed, protected and guided them all safely so far.

Since it was getting late in the day, Christopher decided to anchor offshore and wait until morning before navigating the shoals and reefs that surrounded the island. From all appearances this island seemed just like San Salvador. It had gleaming white sand beaches, and all the flat land was heavily wooded. Christopher hoped that the Indians on the island were as friendly as those on San Salvador had been, and they were. The natives welcomed them and looked happy with the red caps, hawk's bells, and glass beads the sailors gave them.

The wind where the ships had dropped anchor was quite strong, and rather than stay the night there, Christopher decided to sail on in search of a bigger island, hopefully Cipangu (Japan) or, better still, the mainland of Cathay (China).

Later that day a much longer island appeared on the horizon. Christopher immediately named it Fernandina and cautiously sailed closer to it. When Christopher went ashore on Fernandina with some of the crew, he was more impressed with his surroundings than he had been on the other islands. A village was located near the water's edge. It was surrounded by a large garden in which grew a strange variety of grain the natives called *mahiz* (maize). Christopher also kept a lookout for animals, but he saw only parrots and lizards, no sheep, goats, or cows. Several pigs were aboard the *Pinta*, but Christopher decided that they were too valuable aboard ship as a food source to let them loose on the island.

Something else caught Christopher's attention. The natives called it an *amaca* (hammock). It was an ingenious invention—a length of woven cotton strung between two trees and used as a bed. Christopher immediately thought of his crew aboard ship. They would get a much better night's sleep suspended in this kind of bed than they would lying on the hard deck.

As with the other islands Christopher had visited, there appeared to be little gold on Fernandina.

When Christopher inquired of the natives of the island where they might find any, they pointed southward. So Christopher quickly claimed Fernandina for the king and queen of Spain and sailed on.

By now the natives who had been taken captive from San Salvador had become quite adept at communicating with the crew using sign language. Christopher became excited when it was reported to him that the San Salvador Indians had indicated that the source of gold was the land of Colba (Cuba), and especially a village there called Cubanacan. Since the name sounded a lot like great khan, especially if he said it quickly, Christopher convinced himself that Colba was really the mainland of Cathay. Better yet, it was only a couple of days' sailing away.

On the ships sped, zigzagging past islands, which Christopher and his crew named as they encountered, while looking westward for some sign that they were nearing Colba. Finally, on October 28, 1492, a long coastline came into view. Christopher told his crew that this was surely the mainland of Asia, but disappointment awaited them. Instead of discovering the advanced civilization that Christopher had expected to find on the mainland, the crew members who went ashore came back with a description of things that were the same as on the other islands they had encountered—natives who initially fled when the men went ashore, crude thatched huts, and bowls of half-made cassava bread. Although disappointed by these initial findings, Christopher was not yet ready to give up. He summoned his interpreter, Luis de Torres, and a sailor and dispatched them to walk inland until they found a city of great riches. To add weight to the tiny expedition, Christopher handed over the letter of introduction from King Ferdinand and Queen Isabella. The letter, he instructed, was to be given to the great khan as soon as they located him.

The two men set off bravely, and while they were gone, Christopher decided it was time to collect some specimens of local flora and fauna and make repairs to the ships. The men collected many brightly colored parrots, and a group of sailors were able to corner and kill a crocodile, a creature none of them had ever encountered before but which the Indians assured them was a vicious predator who could crush a man in its jaws. The men gutted the crocodile, dried it in the sun to preserve it, and then stuffed it with cotton so that it could be taken back to Spain as a trophy.

The days dragged on until finally the two men returned to the ship. Everyone was eager to hear their report, but alas, the news was not good. Luis reported that not a single person understood Arabic, a fact he could not account for. The men had managed to find a big village of about five hundred huts, but they found no gold there. The people in the village were hospitable, mainly because they seemed to think the two white men were sent to them from the gods.

Luis did have one astonishing fact to report. Many of the inland Indians had a bizarre habit. They lit a roll of leaves, held it to their lips, and sucked in the smoke. Luis reported that the natives appeared to enjoy the sensation of smoking this leaf (which was tobacco), though it was impossible for Christopher or the crew to imagine why.

Describing the way the Indians smoked would make interesting reading for the king and queen in his report, Christopher was sure of that, but it was no substitute for reporting the discovery of large quantities of gold. Once again Christopher decided to sail on. As he left Colba, he renamed the place Juana, after Ferdinand and Isabella's son.

The ships were in good repair on Thursday, November 22, as they sailed away from Juana, with the *Pinta* in the lead and the *Santa María* and *Niña* following. But as the day went on, the *Pinta* got farther and farther ahead of the other two ships until it disappeared over the horizon. Christopher expected Captain Pinzón to tack in a zigzag formation until the other two ships caught him up, but this did not happen. By Friday morning Christopher had to accept the shocking fact that the *Pinta* had deliberately left them behind. Although he stayed outwardly calm at this realization, inside Christopher was seething. He was certain that Martín Pinzón had tired of following orders and had sailed away to search for gold and glory for himself. This left the other two ships in a precarious situation. Now if one of them got into serious difficulties, all of the crew would have to be accommodated on a single ship. Christopher tried not to think much about this possibility, since there was little he could do about it.

The *Santa María* and the *Niña* dropped anchor once more on December 5. By now Christopher was having a difficult time keeping the crews' spirits up. The crew members, too, had expected to encounter great wealth on the voyage, but their hopes of doing so grew dimmer with each passing island.

Christopher knew from the start, however, that this new island they were anchored off, which the local people called Haiti, was special. He renamed the place la Isla Española (the Spanish Isle) and set about writing a description of the place. He had the king and queen in mind as he tried to capture the scene for them:

> In this island there are many harbors on the coast of the sea, incomparable to others which I know in Christendom, and numerous rivers, good and large, which is marvelous. Its lands are elevated and in it there are many sierras and very high mountains.... All are very beautiful, of a thousand shapes, and all accessible and filled with trees of a thousand kinds and tall, and they seem to touch the sky; and I am told that they never lose their foliage, which I can believe, for they are as green and beautiful as they are in Spain in May, and some of them were flowering, some with fruit.... Upcountry there are many mines of metals.

Christopher was not totally sure about that last statement, but he hoped that it was true and that some of those mines produced gold.

Meanwhile Christopher and the crew set about getting to know the local people. On December 16 a local chief was invited aboard the *Santa María* to dine in the captain's cabin. Christopher was very impressed with this leader's solid gold jewelry, which represented one more sign that the explorers were getting closer to the source of the gold in these parts.

As the days went by, more and more Indians visited the ships. On December 22 nearly fifteen hundred natives swarmed aboard the two ships to inspect everything from the nails that held the planks together to the sandbox on deck they used for cooking and the stitching on the by now well-worn sails. Christopher spent many hours observing the visitors, and after they had departed, he mused in his official report,

> To rule here one need only settle and assert authority over the natives, who will carry out whatever they are ordered to do. I, with my crew—barely a handful of men—could conquer all these islands with no resistance whatsoever. The Indians always run away; they have no arms, nor the warring spirit. They are naked and defenseless, hence ready to be given orders and put to work.

Three more days passed, and in that time Christopher learned that the gold on la Isla Española (or Hispaniola, as the name became in English) did not come from mines after all but from gold dust that the natives panned from the rivers.

This was a bitter blow, but Christopher was cheered with reports that there might be more gold on the opposite coast of the island.

During this time a wealthy chief named Guacanagari from an area known as Cibao, situated farther along the northeastern coast of Hispaniola, had sent a gift by messenger to Christopher. The gift was a belt with a buckle formed into a mask, with the tongue, ears, and nose all made of solid gold. Immediately Christopher set out to sail east along the coast to find Guacanagari. However, it was slow sailing as the men battled a head wind. Christopher and the crew were awake for forty-eight hours as they negotiated the treacherous sailing conditions. Finally, by the evening of December 24, Christmas Eve, 1492, they were situated slightly east of Cape Haitien. As they rounded the cape, the head wind dropped and the sea became calm. Realizing that the crew were as exhausted as he was, Christopher ordered the two ships to heave to so that they could spend the night in the shelter of an island just off the shore.

As the sea slopped gently and rhythmically against the side of the *Santa María*, Christopher prepared to get some much-needed sleep, confident that the vessel was in the capable hands of her captain and crew. He had just finished saying his evening prayers and shut his eyes when he heard a bloodcurdling cry. Christopher leaped from his bunk, grabbed his silver dagger, and rushed out onto the deck.

Wrecked

The bloodcurdling scream, Christopher quickly learned, came from the ship's cabin boy manning the tiller one deck below.

"Where's the helmsman?" Christopher snapped down the hatch at the boy.

"He's sleeping," the cabin boy replied, his eyes wild with fright. "He told me to man the helm and not say a thing about it to you in the morning."

"No wonder!" Christopher exclaimed. "I told him to stay at his post through the night. Well, boy, what's all the noise about then?"

"We hit something, sir, and it scared me, and I let out a scream. Now I can't move the tiller," the cabin boy replied.

Grim-faced, Christopher ran to the side of the ship and peered down into the moonlit sea. He could scarcely believe what he saw. It was his worst nightmare come true. The *Santa María* was aground on a coral reef. All Christopher could do was give the order for the crew to abandon ship.

The whole crew made it safely to shore or to the *Niña*. Christopher chose to transfer to the *Niña*, where he paced the deck, waiting anxiously for dawn to break. Despite the damage to the *Santa María*'s hull, he still hoped that on the high tide she might float free of the reef. But the high tide managed to lift the vessel only about six inches, nowhere near enough to float her off the reef. Christopher had to face the fact that the *Santa María* was wrecked. Now the focus became salvaging as much of the ship's cargo and equipment as possible.

The local people aided the Spaniards in their salvage efforts. They worked tirelessly alongside the sailors until almost everything salvageable from the *Santa María* was piled up onto the beach. Much to Christopher's amazement, they did not steal even a glass bead or a lace point. That night Christopher wrote in his report to the king and queen about how impressed he was by the Indians:

> These are loving, tractable and generous people and I swear to Your Highnesses that there are no better people or country on earth. They love their neighbors as themselves, and their speech, it is the gentlest and sweetest in the world; they always speak with a smile. It is true that both men and women go naked as they were born, yet your

Highnesses can believe me that they have very good customs and the king is served with great honor and shows such dignity that it is pleasurable to watch. What good memories these people have, and they are eager to know everything. This moves them to ask many questions about what something is and what it is used for.

With the *Pinta* gone and the *Santa María* wrecked, the expedition had only the *Niña* left. Christopher realized that his Enterprise of the Indies was over. He could not explore further and run the risk of losing the last remaining ship. If the *Niña* were wrecked, there would be no way to get home to Spain, and there would be no rescue mission from there either, since no one knew where they were. Christopher planned to sail for home on the *Niña* as soon as possible, though he was not eager to face the voyage back. It went against everything he knew about good seamanship to set out alone across the Ocean Sea. Such a perilous journey should only be undertaken by two ships to support each other.

As he made preparations to set sail for Spain, Christopher began to wonder whether the wreck of the *Santa María* had just been an unlucky accident, or did God have some other purpose in the disaster? Finally, as a result of the wreck, he decided that God wanted him to establish a colony at this point on Hispaniola. When Christopher told the crew of the *Santa María* his vision, he was surprised at how the men clamored to stay behind on the island. They were eager to be the first to find gold in the Indies and, with it, their fortunes.

Christopher thus gave the order for a fortified camp to be established ashore, which he named Villa de la Navidad (Christmas Town) in honor of the day of the wreck. Planks from the hull of the *Santa María* were used to build the camp. Before long the fortification was finished, and thirty-nine men were chosen to stay behind. Most were from the crew of the *Santa María*, though some were from the *Niña*. Diego de Harana was put in command of Navidad, and Christopher left the men with most of the supplies from the wrecked *Santa María*, as well as her longboat.

On December 31 the Spaniards, along with some of the Indians they invited to celebrate with them, celebrated the arrival of the New Year. And on January 2, 1493, the Indians and the sailors had another celebration, this time a farewell party for the *Niña*.

At sunrise on January 4, the *Niña* sailed from Navidad bound for Spain. Still aboard were the six natives taken captive on San Salvador island. As the ship sailed away, Christopher stood on the poop deck and waved to the men ashore at Villa de la Navidad. He knew that their future was as uncertain as that of the *Niña*'s making it safely back across the Ocean Sea alone. He said a prayer for the men and entrusted them into God's care.

Christopher's plan was to head in a northerly direction until he reached the latitudes where the wind blew from the west. There, when he had estimated that he had reached a latitude equal to Spain, he would turn east and let the westerly wind push him back across the Ocean Sea. However, getting to those northerly latitudes where the favorable winds blew proved to be more difficult than Christopher had imagined. The winds on the north coast of Hispaniola were constantly changing direction or dying away, and it took every bit of Christopher's skill as a sailor to keep the ship moving forward.

Two days after leaving Navidad, as he battled to move the *Niña* forward in the wind, Christopher could hardly believe his eyes when a ship appeared across the horizon. It was the *Pinta*! Christopher had not expected to see the vessel again. As the *Pinta* sailed closer, he felt his anger rising toward Martín Pinzón for deserting the fleet. But by the time the captain of the *Pinta* had rowed over to the *Niña* and climbed aboard, Christopher realized that whatever had happened, he needed to forgive Martín and his crew. The chances for both crews making it back to Spain were much improved if the two ships sailed together and acted as a team.

For his part, Martín apologized for going off in search of gold. He said he had sailed to Great Inagua island to see for himself whether the rumor the Indians told was true, that gold could be picked up on the beaches. Martín reported to Christopher that the rumor had proved to be false. He had then sailed along the coast of Hispaniola and dropped anchor near the Cibao region, where they had found lots of gold. While at anchor there, Martín had heard from the natives of the disaster that had befallen the *Santa María*, and he had set out straightaway to lend a hand to the admiral and his crew.

Together, at midnight on January 8, the *Niña* and the *Pinta* began their homeward journey to Spain. Neither ship was in great condition by now; the ships' sails were worn, and both vessels leaked, keeping their crews busy bailing water from the bilges.

Mile by mile the two ships edged their way north until on the last day of January the wind swung around and began to blow from the west. This was the wind Christopher had been hoping for, but he continued to head north for another four days. Finally, after taking a reading from the North Star, he decided that they were at a latitude that was in line with Spain. He ordered the ships to alter course and head east. Now, with the wind at their backs, the two ships zipped along, and for the next four days they averaged 150 miles per day.

As they sped along, Christopher had no idea that Europe was experiencing one of the coldest and windiest winters ever and that, at that moment, a monstrous, low-pressure storm was howling in the ocean dead ahead. On February 12 both ships ran headlong into the storm. Ferocious crosswinds howled around them, whipping the sea into pyramid-shaped waves that broke over both vessels. The *Niña* was buffeted particularly hard. By now most of the supplies aboard had been used up, and underballasted, the ship pitched and rolled precariously, so much so that Christopher believed she would sink. As a result, Christopher prepared a digest of his journal and sealed it into an old wine cask that was thrown overboard. Christopher hoped that even if the *Niña* sank, his record of the enterprise might find its way to Ferdinand and Isabella.

At the same time that Christopher was preparing his digest, the officers and crew were drawing lots to see who would make a pilgrimage to some famous shrine to the Virgin Mary if she saved them from the storm. But still the wind continued to howl around them, and the waves washed across the deck. The storm became so fierce that the *Pinta* and *Niña* were separated and lost sight of each other completely.

The following day, now alone in the angry ocean, the *Niña* was still afloat. This time all of the crew, including Christopher, vowed together to make a pilgrimage to the first shrine to the Virgin Mary that they encountered if they survived. They vowed to make the pilgrimage wearing only their underwear and shirts. Not long afterward, much to Christopher's relief, the winds began to ease. Then shortly after dawn on February 15, the men finally sighted land straight ahead. Christopher guessed that it was one of the islands of the Azores. However, by now the wind had swung around and was blowing from the east, and it took three days before the battered *Niña* reached the island and dropped anchor. Relief flooded through Christopher when the sails were finally furled.

The island they had reached was Santa María, the southernmost island of the Azores. At the fishing village of Nossa Senhora dos Anjos, close to where the ship lay at anchor, was a church dedicated to the Virgin Mary. As soon as it was practical, the crew, except for Christopher, three seamen, and the six Indians, set out to make their pilgrimage to the shrine, clad only in their long shirts as a sign of penance according to their vow. Christopher and the seamen stayed behind to watch over the ship while the crew were away and determined to make their pilgrimage when the others returned.

On the deck of the *Niña*, Christopher was beginning to wonder why the crew were taking so long on the pilgrimage, when he noticed a boat rowing out toward him from the shore. As the boat approached, a man in it announced himself as the governor of the island and demanded that Christopher surrender to him and be imprisoned with the rest of his crew, who were locked up in the village jail.

The Azores were Portuguese territory, and the arrival of a Spanish ship at the island, according to the governor, could mean only one thing—it was returning from an illicit voyage to West Africa, which was under Portuguese control.

"I can tell you that your notion is misguided," Christopher told the governor. "Neither I nor my ship or crew has been anywhere near the west coast of Africa, and I demand that you release my men, whom you have wrongly imprisoned. I will not, under any circumstances, surrender to you. Nor shall those left aboard this vessel."

"Then you leave me no option but to come aboard your vessel and take you by force," the governor said.

"Permission to board the *Niña* is denied to you. And I myself and those aboard shall resist you with all our effort if you and those with you try to force yourselves aboard. And then I shall go with my remaining men and attack the village and release my crew from captivity."

The governor seemed a little flustered at this and unsure of what to do about the standoff. Christopher was not sure either. But before the impasse could be resolved, a strong and swift gale blew up. The governor headed for the shelter of shore as fast as his men could row, while the *Niña* strained at her anchorline, which eventually snapped, setting the vessel adrift in the rising waves. Thankfully, the wind was blowing from the shore, and the *Niña* was pushed far out to sea and not onto the rocky shore. Soon the island of Santa María sank below the horizon.

Christopher and the three seamen, aided by the Indians, worked frantically to set the sails and gain control over the ship. Eventually they succeeded, and as the gale died down, Christopher was left wondering whether such a skeleton crew could now sail the *Niña* back to Santa María. And if they made it, what awaited them?

Chapter 10

Spain at Last

Two days later, the *Niña* made it back to Santa María island with her exhausted crew. As he dropped anchor once more off the fishing village of Nossa Senhora dos Anjos, Christopher braced himself for a nasty struggle with the island's governor. However, the struggle did not materialize. Christopher soon learned that, during the time the *Niña* had been at sea, the governor had reconsidered his position. After questioning the crew closely, he decided that they were telling the truth, that they were not returning from an illegal trip to the West African coast. As a result, the residents of the island even wanted to restock the ship with provisions for the last leg of her journey back to Spain. Christopher was, of course, relieved at this turn of events.

At daybreak on February 24, her hold generously reprovisioned and a full crew aboard, the *Niña* set sail on the final leg of her return trip to Spain. During the stop in the Azores, Christopher had heard nothing of the fate of the *Pinta*. From what he had learned, she had not stopped at any island in the group, and he decided that she may well have sunk in the storm that separated the two ships.

As the island of Santa María sank from view, everyone aboard the *Niña* hoped that the last twelve hundred miles of their voyage would be uneventful. It was not to be. Once again disaster struck, and the *Niña* found herself in the middle of another huge storm. On the night of March 2, howling winds pulled at the ship, shredding the sails and snapping her masts. When the storm finally passed, the *Niña* was drifting toward the mouth of the Tagus River on the coast of Portugal. Christopher could do little but enter the river and seek refuge in Lisbon, all the while hoping that King John would look kindly on his bedraggled crew. After the *Niña* finally limped into Lisbon and docked, Christopher sent a message to the king announcing his arrival. The king seemed kindly disposed to Christopher and sent back word that he was happy to hear that the *Niña* had returned safely across the Ocean Sea, and he granted Christopher an audience with him.

Soon afterward Christopher, Vicente Yáñez Pinzón, captain of the *Niña*, and three of the Indians set off for a nearby monastery where King John was in the middle of a retreat. The king greeted

Christopher warmly and listened with polite interest as Christopher described the islands of the Indies he had seen. From the king's reaction, Christopher guessed that the king did not really believe that the *Niña* had sailed around the islands of the Indies, and so he ordered the Indians to use some beans to demonstrate the position of their own islands.

As they laid the beans down in a long line, Christopher watched King John's face darken. Then he began to sob. "Why did I let such a prize slip from my hands?" he moaned. "I should have given you the money you asked for and sent you out in the name of Portugal."

Now Christopher was sure that the king believed him, as did the king's advisers who had gathered around to listen.

"You should have this man killed," one of the advisers said to the king. "How dare he come in here bragging about new lands he has discovered for the Spanish crown. Get rid of him and his crew, and the Spaniards will never have to know he returned."

Christopher held his breath as he looked at the king. This was what he had been afraid might happen.

"No, I was the one who passed up this opportunity. We will have to look for another way to remedy it," King John said.

Christopher let out a sigh of relief. His life was safe.

King John asked many more questions about the voyage to the Indies, and Christopher answered most of them as honestly as he could, except the ones about exactly where he had found the Indies; that was something he would reveal only to the Spanish monarchs.

It took eight days to repair the damaged *Niña*. By the time the repairs were complete, another concern was plaguing Christopher. What if the *Pinta* had not sunk? What if she had made it through the storm and had already put into a Spanish port? Would Martín Alonso Pinzón wait for the *Niña* to show up, or would he seek an immediate audience with Ferdinand and Isabella? Christopher knew the answers to these questions. Martín Pinzón was a proud man, and he would gloat over the opportunity to break the news to their Highnesses of reaching the Indies ahead of Christopher. To head off the possibility of such a situation occurring, Christopher sent a message and a copy of his official report overland to the Spanish royal court, explaining where he was and that he was proceeding as fast as he could back to Spain.

On March 13 the *Niña* set sail for home yet again. The following morning when Christopher awoke, the vessel was making her way south along the coast of Portugal near the beach at Lagos, where he had washed ashore after the pirate attack sank the ship he was sailing on seventeen years before. Back then he had prayed that the sinking of his ship would not mark the end of his career as a sailor. Now he was returning to Europe after sailing west all the way to Asia!

The *Niña* sailed on and was soon making her way up the Saltés River. At noon on March 15, 1493, she entered Palos harbor and dropped anchor. It had been seven months and eleven days since the Enterprise of the Indies had set out from this port, and Christopher's heart overflowed with relief and gratitude that he was safely back on Spanish soil. With a flourish Christopher made a final entry in his journal:

> About this voyage, I have observed that the will of God has miraculously been set forth on this voyage, and for myself; who for so long a time was in the court of Your Highnesses, with the opposition and against the opinion of so many people of your household, who were all against me, saying this undertaking was great folly, which I hope in Our Lord will be to the greatest glory of Christianity.

Christopher was hailed as a conquering hero, and the townspeople told him they had never expected to see the *Niña* again.

That evening, much to Christopher's surprise, the *Pinta* sailed into the harbor and dropped anchor! The vessel had not sunk in the storm in the Ocean Sea after all. Christopher soon learned that the *Pinta* had been pushed far north by the storm, causing her to miss the Azores, and that eventually she had reached land at Bayona, near Vigo, in northern Spain. Martín Pinzón explained that he had believed that the *Niña* had sunk in the storm that separated the two ships and that it was his duty to tell the king and queen of the great discoveries the expedition had made in the Indies. He informed Christopher that he had sent a message across Spain to Barcelona, where Ferdinand and Isabella were holding court. In the message he announced his arrival back in Spain and requested an immediate audience to deliver the great news of the success of the expedition. But the king and queen had sent word that they had already received a dispatch from Christopher from Lisbon and would prefer to wait until the *Niña* arrived in Spain and hear about the expedition directly from him.

Christopher was gratified by their Highnesses' response, and the following day he sent off a second official courier to Barcelona with another copy of his report to the king and queen. He also sent a copy of it to Beatriz and his sons, Diego and Ferdinand, in Córdoba so that they would know he had returned safely.

While he waited for a reply from the royal court, Christopher fulfilled the vow he had made in the middle of the storm on the Ocean Sea. He made a pilgrimage to the church of Santa María de la Cinta at Huelva and to the church of Santa Clara de Moguer near Palos. He also went to visit the friars at La Rábida, where he spent several days.

Christopher also spent a great deal of time thinking about the best way to settle the islands he had discovered in the Indies. Before he left Navidad, he had believed that establishing Spanish trading posts in the Indies was the best approach, but now he was having second thoughts. He decided that

Hispaniola should be colonized. To do this, he proposed sending out two thousand Spanish colonists who would build a town in return for being allowed to trade for gold with the Indians in the interior of the island. The gold in turn would be handed over to an official to be smelted, and the king and queen's fifth and his tenth, as well as a tax for the church, be taken from it. Christopher also proposed instituting regular periods when no gold could be traded or searched for, thus forcing the colonists to take the time to plant and tend crops to sustain themselves. In addition, Christopher decided that many priests should be sent to the islands to convert the natives to Christianity and turn them into productive subjects of the Spanish monarchs.

Christopher learned that three weeks after Martín Pinzón arrived back in Palos, Martín had died. Apparently the return voyage had worn Martín out, and he had taken to his bed and died there. Christopher felt little sorrow at his passing; the captain of the *Pinta* had caused him a lot of frustration and trouble on the voyage to the Indies.

On April 7 Christopher received from the king and queen the invitation he had been waiting for. The invitation was addressed to "Don Cristóbal Colón, our Admiral of the Ocean Sea, Viceroy and Governor of the Islands that he has discovered in the Indies." It acknowledged Ferdinand and Isabella's pleasure in Christopher's recent achievement and ordered Christopher to make his way to the royal court in Barcelona as quickly as he could for an audience with them. The king and queen also noted, "It is our wish that that which you have begun with the aid of God be continued and furthered, and we wish to provide you speedily with everything you need to return with His help to the lands which you have discovered."

Christopher was doubly delighted. Not only did the king and queen want an audience with him to officially bestow upon him all the titles and rewards they had promised him if he returned safely, but also they wanted to fund and support another trip to the Indies.

Before he set out for Barcelona, Christopher bought several new sets of clothes in keeping with his new rank and status in Spain. He took with him several of his officers from the voyage as well as the six Indians from San Salvador island. The men were accompanied by a number of servants, valets, two trumpeters, and several militiamen. Christopher organized everyone into a grand procession. The Indians wore their native dress, which consisted of mostly feathers and well-placed gold and fish-bone ornaments. The officers were clothed in new tunics, while Christopher wore black leather boots, a black velvet cloak, and a velvet beret bedecked with parrot feathers. The procession also comprised brightly colored parrots in cages, the stuffed, preserved crocodile, native spears with fish-tooth tips, masks decorated with gold, other native jewelry, a number of gold nuggets, and a hammock, all collected in the islands of the Indies during the expedition. Christopher beamed as he rode along on his white stallion; this was quite a procession, and he was the center of it.

The first stop was Córdoba, where Christopher visited Beatriz, Diego, and Ferdinand. It was a joyous reunion, and Christopher delighted in showing his sons many of the artifacts he had brought back from the Indies and telling them exciting stories of his adventures on the other side of the Ocean Sea.

Christopher took his two sons with him as the procession set out to cover the six hundred miles from Córdoba to Barcelona. As the procession passed through towns and villages, people poured out of their houses to see it go by. Christopher felt honored and dignified as people pointed to him and bowed in respect. Many people joined the procession and walked with it to the next town or village. The procession soon took on the appearance of a traveling carnival, the like of which Spain had never before seen. People particularly wanted to see the crocodile, with its jaws of death.

At each church he passed, Christopher stopped to offer prayers at the altar.

Finally the procession reached Barcelona, and on March 20, 1493, Christopher Columbus was escorted into the grand hall where the sovereigns held court. He held himself erect as he walked. This time he was coming before the king and queen not to beg for money and support for his enterprise but as a returning hero—the man who had crossed the Ocean Sea and found the Indies. Ferdinand and Isabella stood as he entered. When Christopher reached their thrones, he sank to his knees and kissed the back of first the king's hand and then the queen's.

"You may stand," Isabella said.

As Christopher rose to his feet, the queen indicated that she wanted him to be seated in the chair to her right—the seat of honor. Christopher beamed as he lowered himself onto the chair.

After Ferdinand and Isabella had congratulated Christopher on the wonderful success of his Enterprise of the Indies, the six Indians were brought forward and presented to the king and queen, followed by the ship's officers who had made the trip to Barcelona with Christopher. After these formalities had been taken care of, the parrots, the dead crocodile, the hammock, and the other artifacts from the Indies were brought in and presented to their royal Highnesses.

The king and queen then peppered Christopher with questions about the islands he had discovered. Most of Isabella's questions related to the artifacts she had just seen and to the daily lives and religious state of the Indians who lived on the islands. Ferdinand, on the other hand, asked questions about the supply of gold and how Spain could exert her control over the islands and their inhabitants. Christopher did his best to answer their questions as fully as possible.

At the end of the audience, Ferdinand stood and read several letters of nobility that formally conferred on Christopher all the titles, ranks, and rewards promised him if his Enterprise of the Indies proved to be successful. The king also conferred on Christopher a coat of arms.

Before the audience with their Highnesses ended, they all adjourned to the royal chapel, where they chanted a "Te Deum" together. As he chanted the last line, "O Lord, in Thee have I trusted, let me never be confounded," Christopher could not hold back his tears. Thanking God for His blessings to them all seemed like a fitting end to the first voyage.

Christopher walked out of his audience with the king and queen overflowing with gratitude for the way God had raised him up to such an important rank. He had been born the son of a poor weaver in Genoa, had risked everything, and now, as a result, had risen to the highest pinnacle of Spanish society. As hard as it was to believe, he was indeed Don Cristóbal Colón, Admiral of the Ocean Sea, Viceroy and Governor of the Islands he had discovered in the Indies, with his own coat of arms to designate his high social position.

The next event during his stay in Barcelona greatly pleased Christopher. It was the baptism of the six Indians he had brought back from the Indies. The king and queen agreed to act as godparents for the Indians and watched as one was baptized "Ferdinand of Aragon," another "Don Diego," another "Don Juan of Castile," and so on until all six had had holy water sprinkled on them and been given Spanish names. Christopher hoped and prayed that these native men were the first of vast numbers of natives who would embrace Christianity and be baptized. To help this prospect along, he decided that taking a good number of priests on his next trip to the Indies would be a priority. The priests could go forth into the interior of Hispaniola and other islands and convert the natives.

While in Barcelona, Christopher wrote to his brother Bartholomew, who, he learned, was serving in the royal court in France. He invited Bartholomew to become part of the crew on the second voyage to the Indies. He also wrote to his younger brother Giacomo, who was still a weaver in the family business in Genoa, inviting him to come to Spain and join the crew for the second voyage.

As the weeks rolled by in Barcelona, Christopher spent time with the most important people of the city, regaling them for hours with stories of the Indies. Christopher also negotiated with the royal court on the objectives of his second voyage across the Ocean Sea. Eventually Ferdinand and Isabella agreed with Christopher's plan to establish a trading colony on Hispaniola. However, they cautioned that in doing so Christopher needed to be careful to ensure that the natives of the island were treated respectfully and lovingly and that every effort should be taken to convert them to Christianity. To this end the sovereigns decreed that six priests should be appointed to the expedition. As well as being charged with establishing the trading colony, Christopher was charged with further exploring the coast of Colba (Cuba) to discover whether or not it was, in fact, part of the mainland of Asia and could lead the Spaniards to the golden cities of Cathay.

Although Christopher would serve as captain general of the armada for the expedition, he still had matters to take care of. Don Juan de Fonseca, the archdeacon of Seville and a friend of Christopher, was appointed to go to Cádiz and organize the fleet for the voyage.

The most crucial matter to be dealt with before the next expedition to the Indies could get under way was agreeing upon a north-to-south line of demarcation that divided the Ocean Sea. All the lands discovered to the east of this line would be deemed to belong to Portugal, while all discovered lands to the west of it would be Spain's. Christopher suggested that this line be set along the meridian one hundred leagues (318 nautical miles) west of the Azores, because that is where he had noticed a change in conditions on the outbound journey to the Indies. This was the region where the winds blowing west picked up, where a sailor truly left Europe behind.

The final decision for where this line should be drawn on the map was left up to the pope. Finally, on May 4, 1493, the pope issued a bull announcing his decision. He agreed with the Spanish position, setting the line of demarcation one hundred leagues west of the Azores.

Christopher was happy with the decision. Now he could really focus on the expedition ahead. However, he soon learned that King John of Portugal was outraged by the decision and had appealed to the pope to reconsider and shift the line much farther west. Christopher did not think that likely. After all, the pope had been appointed to his position because of the support of Ferdinand and Isabella.

As Christopher was in the final stages of preparations to leave for Cádiz, he was delighted when his brother Giacomo arrived in Barcelona to join the expedition. The two brothers enjoyed a warm reunion, and Christopher confessed his disappointment that as yet he had received no reply from Bartholomew in France.

Christopher had one last matter to deal with before leaving Barcelona—what to do with his two sons. The answer came when Diego and Ferdinand were appointed pages to the royal court and would thus stay on in Barcelona.

With these matters taken care of, Christopher, Giacomo—who had decided to take on the more Spanish name of Diego—and five of the six Indians, whom Isabella allowed to return to the Indies, set out for Cádiz, where the new expedition was marshaling. The sixth Indian, christened Don Juan of Castile, had decided to stay behind and serve in the royal court.

In early July Christopher reached Cádiz, sixty miles down the coast from Palos. The sight that awaited him in the harbor was truly spectacular. Christopher had to admit that Don Juan de Fonseca had done a magnificent job of organizing a fleet for the next voyage to the Indies. Seventeen ships lay at anchor in the harbor, and in Cádiz over twelve hundred sailors, soldiers, and colonists were ready to sail. Fonseca reported that there had been no shortage of men wanting to sign on for the voyage. Christopher could not help but contrast this to the first voyage when he'd had to beg and cajole men to join his crew. De Fonseca also reported that he had purchased all the seeds, plants, implements, tools, livestock, and other such items necessary to founding a colony. He was also busy laying in supplies of food for the journey. Pork and beef were being pickled in brine for the voyage before being loaded aboard the ships. All in all, Christopher was very satisfied with how the preparations were advancing.

As the day of their departure approached, Christopher chose the largest of the seventeen ships to be his flagship for the voyage. He took it as a good omen that the vessel was also named the *Santa María*, as his first flagship had been. The original *Niña* had been refitted and was also set to make the voyage. Christopher was pleased about this. Although the *Niña* was small, he had great faith in her ability to weather the worst storms.

September 25, 1493, dawned a clear, bright autumn day over Cádiz. Christopher had been up since before dawn, making sure that all the last-minute preparations had been taken care of. The wind was light but sufficient, and when he was certain everything was ready, Christopher stood on the poop deck of the *Santa María*, his younger brother Diego (Giacomo) beside him, and ordered anchors aweigh. They were off once again across the Ocean Sea. This time, though, Christopher was not sailing off into the great unknown. At Navidad, Spaniards and friendly Indians were awaiting their return. Christopher hoped that with God's guidance they may have found gold by now and a trove of riches would be waiting for him.

Chapter 11

Back to the Indies

Christopher Columbus was pleased beyond measure as the convoy sailed away from Cádiz. Never had Christopher seen such a splendid sight. High above him on a line that stretched between the tops of the masts hung silken banners bearing the coats of arms of the gentlemen aboard the ships. Christopher's new coat of arms waved brightly with the others. It had the castle of Castile and green lion of Aragon in its upper left and right quarters, a map of islands denoting his discoveries in its bottom left quarter, and five anchors signifying his rank of admiral in the bottom right quarter. Behind his flagship came the others in the convoy, and they were serenaded out into the open sea by a fleet of row galleys from Venice that happened to be in port. And from land came the sound of cannons and music. It was indeed a send-off fit for the admiral of the Ocean Sea. Christopher basked in every moment of it, while above him sailors glided about the rigging like acrobats setting the sails for the voyage west to the Indies.

Seven days later the fleet put in at Grand Canary Island, and then the island of Gomera. They stayed only long enough in each location to stock the ships. Then, on October 12, 1493, one year to the day since first discovering the Indies, the fleet left the Canary Islands and set a course west by south. Christopher Columbus was off on his second voyage across the Ocean Sea.

This time the ocean voyage was nearly perfect. The sea was calm, and the sailors were efficient and experienced. They no longer feared being unable to return to Spain, and they looked forward to making landfall at Navidad. Except for a thunderstorm two weeks out, the weather was sunny and warm, and the ships raced each other during the day. At night they worked their way into a tight formation and would stay together until the morning.

Christopher was delighted with the progress of and planning for the voyage. Surely, he told himself, God had blessed this trip and would crown his efforts with a huge bounty of gold and precious jewels. Even as the ships neared the Indies, Christopher was thinking about the grand entrance he would make upon his return to Spain.

On Sunday, November 3, just twenty-one days after setting sail from the Canary Islands, the cry of "Land! Land!" went up from ship to ship. All hands were instantly on deck, and Christopher led his crew in a round of hymns and prayers to thank God for a short and safe journey.

As the sun rose higher in the sky, a huge landmass took shape on the horizon. Christopher immediately named it Dominica, after the Latin word for Sunday. Christopher scanned the coastline of the island, but seeing no harbor, he ordered the ships to continue on.

Christopher guessed that the wind on the way across the Ocean Sea had brought them farther south than the island of Hispaniola. He adjusted course and began to head in a northwesterly direction. Soon after setting out on this heading, they reached a flat island, which Christopher named Santa María Galante after the sturdy flagship that had carried him safely back across the ocean to the Indies. Nearby they encountered a group of islands that he called Todos Los Santos, since they had celebrated All Saints' Day at sea. On the leeward side of Santa María Galante, Christopher decided to drop anchor. When the ships were all at anchor, he had himself rowed ashore so that he could plant the royal standard and formally take possession of the island for Spain. That done, he took a quick look around the beach. Seeing nothing of value, he reboarded the *Santa María* and again set sail.

The next island they came upon was much larger. Christopher named it Santa María de Guadalupe after one of his favorite shrines and again took possession of it in the name of the king and queen of Spain. Guadalupe was the most beautiful island Christopher had encountered so far, with its towering volcano and silvery waterfall. Many of the crew came ashore at the island, and Christopher gave one of his officers, Diego Marques, permission to hike inland a mile or so with some of the sailors to see what was there.

Christopher soon came to regret that decision, when the men did not return at nightfall. On his last voyage, the natives on Hispaniola had warned him about a tribe of man-eating Carib Indians. Now Christopher feared that they might have landed on their island. As soon as it was daylight, he divided two hundred volunteers into four search parties and sent them out to find the men. They returned that night empty-handed, and the night afterward as well. Just as Christopher was agonizing over what to do next, a search party found the group. They returned to the beach silent and wide-eyed, accompanied by a crowd of young Indians. Christopher took Diego aside to find out what had happened to them.

The facts Christopher learned confirmed his worst nightmares. Diego reported that the jungle inland from the beach was lush and denser than anything the men of the group had encountered before. Soon they had become hopelessly lost and disoriented and began wandering in circles. As they wandered, they made a chilling discovery. The group stumbled upon a hastily deserted village. Diego surmised that they had been spotted by the village inhabitants, who, having never seen white men before, fled in fear. As the men walked around the deserted village, inside the native huts they found cooked human limbs and other cuts of human flesh partially eaten. And when they heard someone whimpering, they followed the sound and discovered two boys penned up like animals and being fattened, to be ready to be eaten at an upcoming feast. The men also found twelve captured girls enslaved in the village.

The men, along with the two native boys and twelve girls, were rowed out to the ships. Once they were all safely aboard, Christopher summoned one of the natives returning from Spain. Using him as an interpreter, Christopher learned that the children were Taínos Indians, captured and carried away when the Caribs raided their village on Hispaniola. Christopher agreed to return the children to their home island.

From the island of Santa María de Guadalupe the ships sailed on, encountering more islands, which Christopher named and claimed in the name of the king and queen of Spain. When they reached one particular island, a native aboard informed Christopher that the island was called Ayay. Unlike most of the islands they had encountered so far, this island was not covered in dense, tropical vegetation. Instead, much of its vegetation had been cleared and the land cultivated so that long, bountiful gardens sloped up from the shore. Christopher decided to rename the island Santa Cruz (St. Croix) and claimed it for Spain.

As the ships sailed along the coast of Santa Cruz, they came to a place where a river flowed into the sea. Beside the river's estuary was located a small Carib village and a large garden. Christopher decided to send a party of men ashore to investigate. He ordered the ships to heave to and drop anchor. The island was surrounded by a reef, which had a small gap that was not big enough for the ships to pass through, so they lay at anchor on the seaward side of the reef.

Christopher chose twenty-five of his best men, made sure they were well armed, and sent them ashore to make contact with the village. From his position on the poop deck of the *Santa María*, Christopher could see the Caribs flee their village when they realized a longboat filled with white men was headed toward them. The Spaniards pulled their boat ashore, and while four of the men guarded it, the others investigated the village. After half an hour ashore, the men set out in their longboat to rejoin the fleet.

As the longboat passed through the gap in the reef, a dugout canoe carrying four Carib men and two women paddled toward the Spaniards. As they approached the longboat, the Caribs drew out their bows and arrows and opened fired on the sailors. Christopher watched helplessly as one of the sailors was struck in the back by an arrow and slumped forward dead, while another was hit in the side and badly wounded. Quickly the Spaniards reversed the direction of the longboat and rammed it into the canoe, sending the Caribs into the water.

Before the sailors could capture their attackers, the Caribs swam to a nearby rock and opened fire on the longboat with another barrage of arrows. This time the Spaniards leveled their crossbows at the Indians and fired back. The Caribs managed to dodge many of their arrows and continued to fight back. Finally an arrow hit one of the Carib men in the abdomen, but still the man fought on. Christopher could scarcely believe how ferociously the Caribs fought. He watched as the native who had been struck in the abdomen jumped into the water and began to swim for shore. The man had almost managed to escape when an arrow from a Spanish crossbow hit him in the back and he finally died.

Since the Spaniards in the longboat outnumbered the Caribs four to one and were better armed, they were finally able to subdue their attackers and take them captive. They bound them hand and foot and brought them back to the ships, where they were manacled below deck.

As the fleet was preparing to sail on, a large group of Caribs, their faces and bodies painted, burst onto the shore, seeking revenge on the Spaniards. But there was little they could do, since they had no weapons powerful enough to fire arrows and other objects out to the ships.

From Santa Cruz, Christopher charted a course more directly west. After discovering and naming still more islands, on November 22, a long coastline appeared on the horizon. This time as they approached, Christopher recognized it as the coast of Hispaniola. He had finally made it. He was back at the large and beautiful island he had discovered on his previous voyage. Christopher was eager to reach Navidad and be reunited with the forty men who had stayed behind eleven months before.

Darkness was descending when the fleet of ships arrived at the pass that led to Caracol Bay and Navidad. As eager as he was to reach the settlement, Christopher did not want to repeat the events of the previous Christmas Eve when the *Santa María* was wrecked on the jagged coral reef. He decided to anchor for the night and proceed into the bay in daylight. However, he ordered flares to be ignited and for the gunner to fire off several cannon shots to let those at Navidad know he had arrived.

To Christopher's great surprise, no response came from those at Navidad. At the very least he had expected that they would fire their cannon as both an acknowledgement of the fleet's arrival and a welcome. Moreover, he had hoped that several of the men might row out to the ships to personally welcome them. The hours passed, and still there was no response. Finally, at midnight, a canoe approached the flagship. When they got close to the ship, the Indians in the canoe called out, "Almirante." Christopher ran to the side of the ship, and when the Indians recognized him, they seemed to let out a sigh of relief. Soon the Indians were standing on the deck of the *Santa María* holding several gifts. Christopher motioned for one of the Indians returning from Spain, who had been baptized in Barcelona as Diego Colón, to come forward and act as interpreter.

Through Diego, the Indians explained that they brought gifts for the admiral from Guacanagari and assured him that things were fine with the Spaniards at Navidad, except that several of the men had died. Christopher thanked them for the gifts and for the information, though he found it odd that they had paddled out to tell him this news and bring him gifts in the middle of the night. Puzzled by this, Christopher left Diego alone with the Indians to see if he could glean any more information from them about the men at Navidad. How had the men died? And had the men discovered the source of gold on the island?

Christopher watched from the poop deck as the Indians, reticent at first to speak openly, began to converse with Diego. An hour passed, and the Indians were still talking to the interpreter. Then another hour passed before an ashen-faced Diego Colón walked over to Christopher.

"What have you learned?" Christopher asked.

"It not good, Almirante, it not good," Diego said.

Christopher's stomach knotted. "What is not good?" he inquired.

Diego began to relate the story the Indians had told him. According to the Indians, the Spanish men at Navidad were unwilling to work. They would not clear any land on which to plant crops, nor would they mine and pan for gold. Instead, they demanded that the Indians give them gold, food, and women. When the Indians could not supply all that the Spaniards demanded, the men formed themselves into small raiding parties and began attacking and looting villages on the island. From these villages, they carried away food and whatever gold they could find, as well as men, women, and children to serve as their slaves. One raiding party attacked a village under the control of Caonabó, the powerful cacique (chief) of the Maguana region in the center of Hispaniola. Incensed by the attack, Caonabó had decided to put an end to the troublesome actions of the Spaniards on the island. He assembled a large group of warriors and attacked Navidad, killing all the white men he found there. He then sent out warriors to track down and kill all the other Spaniards who were dispersed across the island raiding villages.

Guacanagari, Diego explained, had wanted to protect the Spaniards, but compared to Caonabó he was a weak cacique, and he could do little to stop the killing. In fact, Caonabó had killed a number of Guacanagari's people in a small village near Navidad because he suspected that they were cooperating with the Spaniards. That is why Guacanagari had sent gifts to Christopher. He hoped to assuage any anger Christopher might have toward him for failing to stop the killing.

Christopher could scarcely believe what he was hearing. "Are you telling me they are all dead?" he muttered.

Diego nodded silently.

At first light Christopher was rowed ashore. What he found at Navidad confirmed the horrific account of events he had heard the night before. Most of the fort was burned to the ground. At the back of the fort, behind a piece of still-standing stockade made from the timbers of the wrecked *Santa María*, Christopher found eleven badly decomposed bodies. On close inspection of the bodies, he could see that most of their skulls were fractured, indicating that they had been clubbed to death. Try as hard as he might, Christopher could not hold back the tears as he viewed the carnage. He had harbored hopes for Navidad that it would become an important trading outpost for Spain on the north coast of Hispaniola. But it had been turned into a graveyard.

Following the discovery of the bodies, the morale of the crew and colonists aboard the ships of the fleet plummeted. Many of the people began to question whether Christopher had misled them into signing up for the voyage. After all, they argued, they had not seen any gold yet, and the natives were not nearly as friendly as Christopher had portrayed them to be.

Realizing that the situation was quickly deteriorating, Christopher decided that the best thing to do was to find a fresh site for a settlement and begin work on it as soon as possible. He set sail eastward back along the coast of Hispaniola. After battling fierce head winds for twenty-five days and covering only thirty-two miles during that time, he ordered the ships to heave to and drop anchor off a swampy bay. He named the place Isabela after the Spanish queen and immediately ordered that work begin on building a settlement.

In his mind Christopher could see streets, an elaborate church dedicated to the Virgin Mary, and a governor's palace for himself, with an expansive plaza in front of it. But the reality proved to be something quite different. Within a week of beginning work on the settlement, men started getting ill with malaria. Those who did not succumb to the disease complained about the physical labor involved in founding a town on a tropical island. Most of the colonists were not on the government payroll but had paid their own way to the Indies so that they could search for gold and other treasures. Spending hours each day digging ditches and hauling coral stone offended their dignity and made them angry. They became angrier at the sight of the Indians who watched them work. Surely, they told Christopher, the natives could be rounded up, enslaved, and made to do all the work.

At first Christopher resisted this idea and allowed a search party to go out looking for gold. He instructed the group to head inland, where one of the chiefs had told him that gold nuggets lay on the ground. The group, consisting of about twenty Spaniards and an equal number of Indian guides, soon set out. When they returned to Isabela, they brought good news in the form of three large gold nuggets and the promise of much more as soon as mining parties could be arranged.

The discovery of the gold was a tremendous relief to Christopher, as he was preparing to send twelve of the ships back to Spain for more supplies. Now, as well as asking for medicine, food, and clothing for the settlement, he had evidence that the settlement would soon become a source of considerable income for the king and queen.

Along with a letter to Ferdinand and Isabella and the gold, Christopher sent back to Spain sixty parrots and twenty-six Caribs the men had captured.

He was eager for the church to convert and baptize these natives so that in the future they could become useful interpreters in Spain's efforts to rule over the islands of the Indies.

Following the departure of the twelve ships for Spain, tempers settled and work continued on the building of Isabela.

A month after the ships left, Christopher decided to organize and lead a reconnaissance trip inland. On March 12, 1494, several hundred men clad in metal breastplates and helmets headed inland south from Isabela. They marched in formation and were accompanied by drummers and trumpeters and carried banners. Even Christopher had to admit to himself what an unlikely sight they were as they marched off into the dense tropical jungle.

The group crossed the mountains by a pass and descended into a broad valley. Christopher was deeply moved by the beauty of the valley, which he named Vega Real (Royal Plain). In Vega Real the men marched amid fields of maize and through stands of mahogany, ebony, and silk-cotton trees. Small native villages dotted the valley, and their residents brought small packets of gold to the men as they passed.

The group marched on, crossing the Rio Yaque del Norte on rafts and in canoes and heading up onto a mesa that overlooked a bend in the Rio Janico. There, under the leadership of Pedro Margarit, one of his lieutenants, Christopher left fifty men to build an earthen fort. The others marched on a little farther into the mountains, where they prospected for gold, collecting a reasonable amount of the precious metal in the process. Although it rained nearly every day, the gold seemed to take the men's minds off the weather.

After twenty-nine days away, Christopher led the group back to Isabela, leaving the fifty men behind to man the earthen fort they had built and had named Santo Tomás. Once he arrived back at Isabela, Christopher sent four hundred men under the command of Alonso de Hojeda to relieve Pedro Margarit and his men at Santo Tomás and to continue exploring the central region of Hispaniola. Before the men left, Christopher gave Hojeda permission to require the Indians that they passed to give them food and water, but he reminded him that it was Ferdinand and Isabella's express wish that the Indians be treated with courtesy and respect in the hope that they would become baptized Christian converts.

After the men had left, Christopher felt restless. He wanted to continue on with his exploration of the islands of the Indies. He felt sure that the mainland of Cathay (China) was only a few days' sail away, and he was eager to find it. Christopher decided to leave his brother Diego in charge of Isabela while he set sail again to explore farther west. For this trip Christopher made the *Niña* his flagship, and it was accompanied by two smaller vessels, the *San Juan* and *Cardera*. Together the three ships had a total crew of sixty men, and with Providence on their side, Christopher hoped that they might soon all be standing on the Asian continent.

Chapter 12

Trouble on Hispaniola

The three caravels, *Niña*, *San Juan*, and *Cardera*, left Isabela on April 24, 1494, and sailed westward along the north coast of Hispaniola. Five days later they crossed the Windward Passage that divided Hispaniola and Colba (Cuba) and reached Cape Maisi, Colba's most easterly point. Since, on his first voyage to Colba, Christopher had explored along the north coast, he decided this time to make his way along the southern coast.

On the last day of April the three ships sailed into a large, semicircular bay that Christopher named Puerto Grande. Beside the beach in the bay they spotted a Guantánamo Indian village. Christopher sent a party of men ashore to greet the Indians and trade with them. When the Indians saw the white men approaching in their longboat, they abandoned their village and fled into the jungle.

Seeing this from the ship, Christopher was rowed ashore to assess the situation for himself. He found a huge dinner the Indians had been preparing still roasting over the fire. The meal consisted of fish, iguana, and hutia (a large native rodent). Diego Colón, the Indian translator, was eventually able to talk the cooks into coming back to finish cooking the meal and share it with their Spanish guests.

Christopher sat with the chief as they ate. He was amused to see that his men enjoyed the hutia, but not one of them would touch the roasted iguana. He noted, though, that the Guantánamo Indians did not seem to mind, as they relished iguana meat, and this left more for them.

Following the feast Christopher made sure that the Indians were thanked for their hospitality with hawk's bells and other trinkets. On the high tide the next morning the three ships sailed out of Puerto Grande and resumed their course westward along the coast. During the night, word about the Spaniards had spread among the Indians living on the coast. When the ships sailed by, hundreds of Indians flocked to the shore to see the men who, they believed, had come down from the sky, and urged them to stop awhile at their village. When the Spaniards did not come ashore, the Indians would clamber into their canoes and paddle out to the ships. Christopher ordered that the Indians were to be well treated, and the Indians all left happily with hawk's bells, glass beads, and other items the Spaniards gave them.

The *Niña*, *San Juan*, and *Cardera* sailed on until they reached Cabo de Cruz. But instead of turning north here into the Gulf of Guacanayabo and following the coast of Colba, Christopher decided to head south in search of the island some of the Indians along the coast had told him about. The island was called Jamesque (Jamaica), and Christopher hoped it would yield a lot of gold.

The winds blew up, churning the sea and causing the ships to pitch and roll as they headed south. On May 5 the ships eventually reached the north coast of Jamesque and anchored in a bay that Christopher named Santa Gloria. Christopher was so captivated by the beauty of the island of Jamesque that he declared it to be the most beautiful island he had discovered in the Indies so far. However, while he was admiring the scenery from the deck of the *Niña*, about seventy native warriors in large dugout canoes came paddling toward them. Christopher thought they looked like a war party and ordered the cannon to be fired over their heads. Soon the natives were paddling back toward the beach at top speed.

From Santa Gloria the ships made their way west along the north coast of Jamesque until they came to Rio Bueno, another harbor. Once again a group of threatening warriors paddled out to the ships in their canoes, but this time the cannon fire did not frighten them off. Christopher ordered his men to open fire with crossbows. Several of the natives were hit and killed with arrows from the crossbows before the attackers retreated.

By now the water supply aboard the ships was getting low, and Christopher sent a landing party ashore with the water barrels. Overwhelmed by the party's crossbows, swords, and fierce dogs, the Indians soon supplied the sailors with food and water and other provisions for their journey. Despite repeated demands from Christopher, however, they could produce no gold.

After the water barrels had been refilled and loaded back aboard the ships, along with the other provisions the Indians had supplied, the small fleet sailed on to Montego Bay. Disappointed that Jamesque did not seem to have the abundant supply of gold he was hoping for, at Montego Bay Christopher ordered the ships to set course north back to Colba.

Three days later the vessels passed Cabo de Cruz and sailed into the Gulf of Guacanayabo, where they continued their exploration of Colba's coastline. As they sailed along, Christopher was constantly on the lookout for anyone who might look vaguely like someone from Cathay (China). Surely by now, he reasoned, if this were truly the mainland of Cathay, there ought to be evidence of its people and culture. But try as he might to find this evidence in Colba, Christopher could not. Everywhere the ships sailed and explored, the men found more Indians living in small villages and no sign of the great khan's advanced civilization overflowing with gold and other precious commodities that Marco Polo had described seeing. Christopher began to wonder whether Colba might be just another island like Hispaniola and the other islands he had discovered so far. Perhaps it was not a peninsula attached to the mainland of Cathay. But Colba seemed too long to be just another island. Christopher reasoned that they had been sailing along her south coast for days now and had found no sign of the western end of an island.

Christopher's suspicions about Colba's being an island and not a peninsula were further allayed when a group of Indians told him that the name of the region was called Magón. To Christopher this sounded very close to Mangi, the province of Cathay that Marco Polo had described in some detail in his book. He told himself they were in Cathay after all!

Finally, as they kept moving westward, they reached a point where Taíno Indians faded away. Now the villages they encountered were populated by Siboney Indians. Because Diego Colón, the Indian interpreter, could not understand their language, communication was once again reduced to hand signals and gestures.

Christopher wanted to keep heading west, but by now his ships were starting to leak, and their sails were showing serious signs of wear. It was time to start heading back to Isabela. However, before he gave the order for the ships to come about, Christopher had each man on his crew sign a statement that declared Colba to be part of the continent of Asia, since no island of that length could exist. Therefore, the statement said, it was pointless to sail any farther west to prove the point.

With the statements signed, Christopher gave the order to come about, and on June 13, 1494, the three ships began their journey back to Isabela. It was a slow and arduous trip. The ships were now sailing into a head wind as well as having to fight the strong current that flowed westward. To avoid the force of the current and to pick up the breezes that blew from the island, Christopher had the ships sail in the still water close to shore. This in turn meant that he and the captains of the three ships had to be particularly vigilant as they navigated their way among shoals and around rocks and coral outcrops.

By July 18 they had reached Cabo de Cruz, and once more Christopher decided to head south to Jamesque. Three days later the ships sailed back into Montego Bay and dropped anchor. From Montego Bay they made their way around the western tip of the island and explored the south coast of Jamesque. Each night the three vessels put into a small bay or harbor and dropped anchor. Although he posted guards each night, Christopher was relieved that no more canoes filled with warriors tried to storm the ships. On August 19 they sailed past Morant Point, Jamesque's eastern cape, and crossed the Windward Passage, arriving on the south coast of Hispaniola.

The ships followed the south coast of Hispaniola, stopping to explore bays and harbors as they went. Christopher was particularly struck by some of the places they stopped at. The places were much better sites for future towns and trading posts than anything he had seen on the northern coast of the island. Finally the ships rounded the eastern tip of Hispaniola and headed west toward Isabela, where the *Niña*, *San Juan*, and *Cardera* dropped anchor on September 19, 1494.

At Isabela a pleasant surprise awaited Christopher. When he stepped ashore, his brother Bartholomew greeted him. The two brothers enjoyed a wonderful reunion. Bartholomew explained that the letter Christopher had written inviting him to join the second voyage to the Indies had never reached Paris. However, news of Christopher's success in finding the Indies did finally reach France, and when he heard it, Bartholomew set out right away for Barcelona. He arrived too late and learned that the fleet of ships had already sailed from Cádiz on the second voyage. But Bartholomew was given an audience with Ferdinand and Isabella, who were so impressed with him that they offered him the command of three caravels to bring fresh supplies to his brother on Hispaniola. Bartholomew had jumped at the opportunity, and now, as a result, the three Columbus brothers were together again.

As good as it was to be reunited with Bartholomew, Christopher was soon confronted with the disastrous situation that had befallen Isabela. Diego Columbus had proved to be an ineffectual leader. While Christopher had been exploring the coast of Colba, Pedro Margarit and about 250 well-armed Spaniards had been roaming through the interior of Hispaniola, plundering Indian villages as they went. When Diego heard what was happening, he sent word immediately ordering Margarit to cease harassing the Indians and to return to Isabela with his men. Instead, Margarit and his men marched on Isabela. They stormed into the settlement, where Margarit told Diego that he was incensed that a Genoese would try to order him, a loyal Spaniard, around, and he demanded the order be withdrawn. When Diego refused to withdraw the order, Margarit and his men linked up with other malcontents in the settlement, among them Fray Buil, one of the priests sent out by Ferdinand and Isabella to evangelize the natives. Fray Buil, however, had not as yet managed to convert even one of the natives and proved himself to be more adept at stirring up trouble among the colonists at Isabela. Together, this combined group of renegade soldiers and malcontents stormed the three caravels Bartholomew had recently arrived with and set sail in them for Spain. Fray Buil had informed Diego before he left that he and Margarit would be sure to give the sovereigns a full and complete report on the incompetence and mismanagement of the colony by the Columbus brothers.

Now, on his return to Isabela, Christopher felt the full weight of the resentment of the colonists heaped on him and his brothers. The colonists accused him of lying to them about conditions on Hispaniola and about the amount of gold that could be found on the island, and they wanted to get some revenge on Christopher.

Two months after arriving back at Isabela, Christopher was still pondering what do about the situation. Also around this time, four caravels carrying supplies and under the command of Antonio de Torres arrived from Spain. Along with the supplies that the ships brought came a letter for Christopher from the king and queen.

By now Christopher supposed that the sovereigns had heard an earful of complaints about him and his leadership. He opened the letter with trepidation. To his surprise Ferdinand and Isabella were very cordial toward him in the letter, though they urged him to leave Hispaniola under the leadership of his brother or some other suitable person and return to Spain.

Christopher did not feel that the time was right for him to return to Spain. He still had much to do in making sure that things on Hispaniola were put on a good footing. As a result, he now had two problems to deal with—placating the king and queen for not immediately returning home, and dealing with the colonists. The answer to these dual problems soon came to him—slaves. Christopher decided that shipping home several hundred Indian slaves would soothe any worries the king and queen might have about his ability to get the job done on Hispaniola. And hadn't the colonists been complaining about the amount of work involved in establishing the colony almost from the first day they arrived? Why not let them have slaves as well to lessen the burden? Christopher gave orders for the colonists to go inland and enslave two thousand Indians. It did not take the colonists long to carry out his orders, and soon two thousand Indians were penned up at Isabela.

At the end of February 1495 Antonio de Torres was ready to sail the four caravels back to Spain. Before he left, five hundred Indian slaves, all that the vessels could hold, were loaded aboard and soon were on their way across the Ocean Sea.

Once the caravels had left for Spain, Christopher allowed the colonists to take the Indians who were left to serve as their slaves. As he had hoped, this pleased the colonists greatly, though it did not induce them to use the slaves wisely, clearing land and planting crops. As a result, the residents of Isabela remained dependent on the flow of supplies that now arrived periodically from Spain.

Several of the Indians who had been penned up at Isabela had managed to escape. One of them was a cacique named Guatiguaná, who immediately headed inland and tried to unite the Indians against the Spaniards. Christopher first learned of Guatiguaná's plan when several Indians came to Isabela and informed him that a large army of warriors had amassed at Vega Real and were preparing to attack the Spanish settlement and kill everyone in the place. Alarmed by the report, Christopher knew that he needed to act quickly. He decided to take the offensive. Rather than wait for the Indians to reach Isabela, he would march inland and attack them.

Christopher, Bartholomew, and Alonso de Hojeda led two hundred armor-clad Spaniards inland. Twenty of the soldiers rode on horses, and they had twenty hound dogs with them, all of which had been shipped to Isabela several months before. Many of the soldiers carried arquebusses, primitive flintlock muskets. Sure enough, near Vega Real they came upon the massed Indian warriors. Hojeda led the horsemen in a charge as he unleashed the savage dogs. Apart from those who may have visited Isabela, the Indians of Hispaniola had never seen horses or dogs before. And as the horses crashed in among the huddled warriors and the dogs attacked them, the assembled mass of Indians began to flee even before the other soldiers could fire off their arquebusses. The Indians fled in all directions, completely routed and demoralized.

With the defeat of the assembled Indian army, it was clear to everybody who now controlled Hispaniola. Christopher decided it was time to press the advantage. Since the Spaniards were not receiving the amount of gold they had hoped through trading with the Indians, he introduced a tribute system. He declared that every native over fourteen years of age was required to pay four hawk's bells full of gold dust to the Spanish every year, and the caciques were required to turn over considerably more gold dust every month to the Spanish.

Satisfied with his conquest of Hispaniola and feeling that things were back on track with colonizing the island, Christopher began to think it might be time to return to Spain. He decided to appoint Bartholomew leader of the colony in his absence. He also charged his brother to find a suitable site and build a new settlement on the south coast of Hispaniola and abandon low-lying, swampy, disease-plagued Isabela.

On March 10, 1496, Christopher boarded the *Niña* for the voyage back to Spain. Accompanying the *Niña* was a fifty-ton caravel named *India*. This vessel had been built at Isabela with timber from the *San Juan* and *Cardera*, which had accompanied Christopher on the exploration of the coast of Colba. Both the *San Juan* and *Cardera* had been swamped and had sunk in a hurricane that swept through the area several months before. Aboard the *Niña* and *India* were 225 Spaniards and 30 Indian slaves. Because the ships had been built to accommodate a crew of fifty, they were cramped and overcrowded.

With so many people aboard, a month out from Hispaniola, Christopher was forced to reduce daily rations so that each person aboard received six ounces of cassava bread and a cup of water a day.

Finally, on June 11, 1496, the two ships reached Cádiz, ending Christopher's second trip to the Indies. Two years and nine months had passed since he had set sail from Cádiz, and his arrival home was far less grand than his departure. Every available flag and banner had been hoisted on the ships, which nevertheless were a bedraggled sight to behold. Those aboard were barely alive. Their eyes were sunken and their skin yellowed, and many of them, including Christopher, needed assistance getting ashore. Christopher had a high fever and was suffering from arthritis, which made it painful for him to walk. Still, he was grateful that he had made it safely back to Spain. He intended, as soon as he was well enough, to make his way to the royal court and give Ferdinand and Isabella a full report on his trip and, if need be, defend his actions on Hispaniola.

Chapter 13

Humiliation

O nce the *Niña* and *India* had anchored in Cádiz harbor and the sailors had dispersed, Christopher made his way to the home of his friend Father Andrés Bernaldez to recuperate and wait for a royal summons. He dreaded meeting with Ferdinand and Isabella, as he was sure his detractors had been hard at work blackening his name. Staying with Father Bernaldez provided Christopher with plenty of time to think about what had gone wrong in the Indies. At first he blamed his misfortunes on other people, but slowly he came around to thinking that God was punishing him because he had become too proud of his new titles and role. Once convinced of this, Christopher decided to change his behavior. He asked to borrow the garb of a Franciscan monk and wore the brown robe instead of his usual showy clothes. The robe was itchy and hot, but it fit Christopher's mood, and Christopher felt that wearing it would show God how penitent he was.

Waiting to be summoned for an audience at the royal court dragged on, as the king and queen were involved in planning the weddings of three of their children. The first, and most important for Spain, was the marriage of their son, Crown Prince Don Juan, to the daughter of the emperor of Austria. As well, their daughter, Princess Doña Juana, was marrying the son of the same emperor, while another daughter was marrying King Don Manuel, the new king of Portugal. To prepare for the weddings, the court had moved to Burgos, the capital of Old Castile. In many ways Christopher was glad that the weddings were distracting the sovereigns from his plight. It gave him more time to pray and think about how best to handle the personal attacks that he knew would come from Fray Buil, Pedro Margarit, and others who had returned from Hispaniola.

Two months passed before Christopher received word that the king and queen were ready to receive him. For the second time, Christopher arranged a cavalcade of Indians and their artifacts. Unlike the cavalcade after the return from his first voyage to the Indies, this one did not draw the same admiring crowds along the way. It was yet another reminder to Christopher of how fleeting being a national hero could be.

Once he arrived at the court, Christopher received a mixed reaction. His two sons, Ferdinand and Diego, as well as the king and queen, were glad to see him. But many of the courtiers were not. They whispered behind his back and taunted him with the title, "Admiral of the Mosquitoes."

Queen Isabella expressed surprise at seeing Christopher in the garb of a Franciscan monk, and Christopher took the opportunity to explain to their royal Highnesses that he had done a lot of soul searching about his role in the difficulties those on Hispaniola had faced. He then asked to be sent back to the island so that he could take over the governorship of the place once again and explore more of the Indies.

Ferdinand and Isabella did not immediately concede to this request. In fact, it took five more audiences with the king and queen over a period of more than a year before they agreed to outfit Christopher on yet another voyage. The delay in approving a third trip to the Indies was due in part to a series of personal tragedies that had befallen the royal household. In 1497, soon after his marriage, their only son, Crown Prince Don Juan, had died. Then a year later their daughter Isabella, who had become the queen of Portugal, died in childbirth.

Christopher knew that Ferdinand and Isabella's sponsorship of a third voyage to the Indies was spurred not by their faith in him but because other monarchs were also planning voyages of discovery. The Portuguese king, the Spanish sovereigns' son-in-law, was preparing to send off Vasco da Gama on a trip around the Cape of Good Hope to India, while King Henry VII of England was rumored to be sending out a fleet of adventurers to explore across the ocean.

The king insisted that the fleet sailing to the Indies be smaller than the previous one. He authorized Christopher to recruit three hundred men and thirty women to make the voyage with him. But recruiting these people proved extremely difficult. Everyone now knew about the harsh conditions on Hispaniola and the way the Indies had turned from a friendly place to a death trap.

Christopher complained to the king and queen about the trouble he was having recruiting a crew for the voyage. In turn the king and queen obligingly decreed that any convict who signed to go to Hispaniola for two years would be pardoned and set free from jail. Even so, it still took a long time to get the men, women, and supplies needed for another voyage.

It was not until May 1498, nearly two years after returning to Spain, that Christopher finally set sail again for the Indies. This time six ships were in the convoy. Three of them were to head straight for Hispaniola, while the other three ships under Christopher's command would set sail on a more southerly course. While back in Spain, Christopher had reread Aristotle and reacquainted himself with the ancient Greek philosopher's adage that the farther south you sailed, the more gold and other precious items you were likely to find. This had been the experience of the Portuguese as they explored farther and farther south down the coast of Africa. With this in mind, Christopher hoped that his three ships would discover the vast quantities of gold they sought closer to the equator. After exploring in this region, he would then sail on to Hispaniola to join up with the new band of settlers traveling on the other three ships.

The six ships sailed together as far as the Canary Islands, where they took on more food and water. Then the ships separated, with Christopher setting course with his three caravels, his flagship *La Nao*, *Correo*, and *Vaqueños*, for the Cape Verde Islands. At first the winds were behind them, and they covered 750 miles in six days. Then disaster struck: the three ships were becalmed on a glassy sea.

Day after day the vessels drifted with no wind in their sails. The weather was stifling hot, and the crew began to panic. Christopher tried to calm them, but even he was beginning to have doubts as to whether they would ever move again. He had never been becalmed for more than a few hours at a time before. He called for special prayer meetings and dedicated the mission to the Holy Trinity. Finally, after nine days, the wind whipped up again, and the three ships were off on their way under full sail.

The rest of the voyage was uneventful, and on the last day of July 1498 the welcome cry of "Land! Land! Three hills dead ahead!" went up from the lookout. Christopher scrambled up the rigging on the mainmast for a better view. Sure enough, three hills broke the horizon. "Trinidad ahead!" Christopher yelled, naming the landfall after the Holy Trinity, whom he credited with bringing the ships safely to this point.

As the island got closer, Christopher gave the order to sail along its south coast, looking for a river mouth as they went. When they found one, the three ships dropped anchor. Once the sails were furled, the men went ashore, stripped, and washed themselves and their clothes in the fresh water of the river. For the next three days, as Christopher and his men rested, they kept an eye out for natives. Christopher assumed that the people they encountered would either be black, like those who lived at the same latitude in Africa, or be like those from Cathay (China). He was a little annoyed when, instead, a canoeload of Indians like those on Hispaniola paddled up beside the ship. The Indians were not the people he had expected to find.

Hoping to interest the natives in trade, Christopher ordered metal trinkets to be displayed on the deck. Some of the Indians climbed aboard ship, but they were not impressed with the items. To try to pique their interest, Christopher told the cabin boy to dance while one of the sailors played the pipes. Instead of enjoying the display, the Indians yelled and ran for their canoe. Once they were aboard it, they pulled out arrows and fired a volley of them at the ships. Christopher concluded that they must have thought the cabin boy's jig was a war dance. He made a note to himself not to try that approach again.

After the period of rest, the three ships sailed on through a narrow, swift-flowing strait, which Christopher named Boca de la Sierpe (Mouth of the Serpent). From there they sailed across the Gulf of

Paria. When they reached land on the other side of the gulf, Christopher assumed that they had reached another island. He led some of his men ashore to replenish their supply of fresh water, unaware that this was the first time a European had set foot on the South American continent.

One of the caravels was sent on ahead to explore, and it returned several days later with interesting news. The crew had discovered the four mouths of a huge river system (the Orinoco); one was so big that it created a channel of fresh water that extended out to sea for twenty miles.

Christopher was astonished at the news. He could think of only one logical reason for such a large volume of fresh water: the water must flow from a very large landmass. Then he enthusiastically recalled that he had dedicated this particular voyage to the Holy Trinity. After taking some time to read the book of Genesis, he concluded that the Father, Son, and Holy Spirit had guided him to that most holy of places—the Garden of Eden. He later outlined his reasons for coming to this conclusion in a letter to be sent back to Ferdinand and Isabella.

> The Scriptures tell us that in the Earthly Paradise grows a tree of life, and that from it flows the source that gives rise to the four great rivers, the Ganges, the Tigris, the Euphrates, and the Nile. The Earthly Paradise, which no one can reach except by the will of God, lies at the end of the Orient. And that is where we are....

It would be the greatest thing for Spain to have a revenue from this undertaking; Your Highnesses could leave nothing of greater memory.... And Your Highnesses will gain these vast lands, which are an *Other World*, and where Christianity will have so much enjoyment, and our faith in time so great an increase. I say this with very honest intent and because I desire that Your Highnesses may be the greatest lords in the world, lords of it all, I say; and that all may be with much service to and satisfaction of the Holy Trinity.

Christopher felt, however, that this was not the time to explore the "Garden of Eden." He needed to sail on to Hispaniola as soon as possible to see how Bartholomew and the little colony had fared and whether the three other caravels had arrived safely.

Before they began to head north toward Hispaniola, the ships sailed on to the west. They stopped at an island that Christopher named Margarita, which meant pearl in Spanish. He named it this because the bays of the island were littered with pearl oyster beds. However, since Christopher was in a hurry to move on, he made a note in his journal to return to the island as soon as possible to explore further.

The three caravels made their way toward the south coast of Hispaniola. In a letter from Bartholomew to him while he was in Spain, Christopher had learned that his brother had found a suitable site with a sheltered harbor for a new settlement. Bartholomew had named the new settlement Santo Domingo, after their father. Christopher was eager to see Santo Domingo, yet as he approached Hispaniola, a sense of dread overcame him. Would his brothers be there to meet him? What if the community had been attacked by Indians and its residents massacred? What would he tell their royal Highnesses then?

As *La Nao, Correo,* and *Vaqueños* entered the harbor and dropped their anchors on August 31, 1498, Christopher was relieved to see that Santo Domingo was still there. But his joy was short-lived when he heard what had happened in the more than two years he had been away. The problem had arisen not between the Indians and the Spaniards but among the Spaniards themselves.

Francisco Roldán, whom Christopher had previously appointed as chief justice of the colony, had led a rebellion against Bartholomew. As improbable as it seemed to Christopher, Roldán had managed to convince one hundred Spaniards to escape inland with him. There they had joined forces with some Indians and returned to attack Santo Domingo several times. They had even tried to seize the three caravels recently arrived from Spain and recruit the sailors on them to take them home.

This was a serious breach of trust, and Christopher wanted to punish Roldán and those who had joined in his rebellion for their disobedience. However, he realized that doing so could easily cause more trouble for them all. After all, they were a comparatively small group of Europeans perched on a small island on the other side of the Ocean Sea. If they continued fighting each other, who could say whether any of them would survive to tell the tale? Over Bartholomew's objections, Christopher called for a meeting with the rebel leader. He and Roldán met in the jungle behind Santo Domingo, where they reached a compromise. Christopher promised to provide two vessels for any of the rebels who wanted to return home to Spain and a pardon to those who wanted to stay on at the community. In addition, he promised to give each rebel who stayed his own plot of land and the ownership of all the Indians who lived on it.

With these odious concessions behind him, Christopher hoped that the settlement would grow and prosper. But it was still filled with problems. Christopher, Bartholomew, and Diego struggled on as the leaders of the colony, but the tide of defiance against the "three foreign Genoese" kept rising, so much so that they felt it necessary to hang several rebels in order to keep the peace, enforce the law, and assert their leadership. By the time the summer of 1499 rolled around, Christopher was particularly concerned about the reports that would probably have reached the Spanish royal court by then. However, he could do little about the situation except hope and pray that the king and queen would remain loyal to him.

When a fleet of caravels sailed into Santa Domingo harbor in August 1500, Christopher's hopes were dashed. Aboard one of the caravels was Francisco de Bobadilla, a royal representative who had been sent to investigate the situation on Hispaniola. Christopher was incensed to learn that Bobadilla carried with him an official document granting him complete authority over the island.

A new rebellion was in progress at the time Bobadilla arrived, and in an effort to contain it, Diego Columbus had ordered that two of the rebels be hanged. Five more were lined up to be hanged when Bobadilla stepped ashore. Bobadilla was aghast at what he saw happening in the name of the king and queen of Spain, and he took immediate charge of the situation. He ordered that the prisoners waiting to be executed be released, and in their stead he ordered that Christopher, Bartholomew, and Diego Columbus be fettered and imprisoned. He also confiscated all of Christopher's gold, maps, journals, and other personal property.

The three brothers sat in the prison at Santo Domingo, pondering their fate. At first Christopher could not believe this was happening to him. But as the fetters and chains bit into his wrists and ankles, he was forced to accept that he, Admiral of the Ocean Sea and Governor and Viceroy of the islands he had discovered in the Indies, was being treated no better than a dog. If only he could talk to Queen Isabella in person, everything would be all right then, he was sure of that. The queen, more than anyone else in the world, understood his good intentions and the horror of his present situation.

As it happened, Christopher got his wish. Bobadilla decided to send the three Columbus brothers back to Spain to stand trial for the violence and death that had occurred under their leadership.

Bartholomew was loaded aboard one caravel, and Christopher and Diego onto *La Gorda*. Christopher was in agony throughout most of the trip back to Spain. The fetters turned the flesh on his wrists and ankles to shreds, and eventually the captain of *La Gorda* took pity on him and offered to remove the fetters. However, Christopher refused the offer. "It is by the order of the sovereigns that I have been placed in chains, and I shall wear them until the sovereigns themselves order that they be removed," he told the captain.

The ships made a speedy crossing of the Ocean Sea and arrived in Cádiz in late October 1500. Christopher disembarked ship in his fetters and was taken to Seville to stay in a monastery until the king and queen decided what to do with him.

While staying at the monastery, Christopher decided to write to Queen Isabella to tell his side of the story. He was sure that she would understand. He told her of the humiliation he had endured being returned to Spain in fetters and asked her to punish the rebellious men on Hispaniola who had conspired against his leadership and that of his brothers, causing them much trouble and heartache. After all, he had been trying his best to uphold their Highnesses' rights in Hispaniola. He also pointed out that like the queen, he was a faithful servant of God. "Our Lord made me the messenger and showed me the way to the new heaven and earth," he declared. He ended his letter by saying, "Our Lord God still exists in His power of old, and He will punish all in the end, especially the ingratitude of injuries."

Christopher knew that if he dispatched his letter directly to the royal court, it was unlikely to get delivered to Queen Isabella. Many royal courtiers despised Christopher, who knew that if the letter found its way into their hands, they would not pass it on. Instead, he sent the letter to Juana de Torres, who had been a court nurse to Ferdinand and Isabella's children. Juana was also the sister of Antonio de Torres, captain of one of the ships on the second voyage to the Indies. She had a rapport with the queen and undertook to get Christopher's letter privately into her hands.

It was not long before Christopher learned that upon reading his letter, Ferdinand and Isabella were perplexed at how he had been treated and that he had been returned to Spain in fetters. They ordered the fetters removed immediately and sent Christopher two thousand ducats for him to buy some new clothes so that "he could appear in court in a state befitting a person of his rank."

It felt good to Christopher when the fetters were finally removed from his ankles and wrists. Although the fetters were gone, they had left deep scars that for the rest of his life would remind him of his humiliating treatment. Still, he was now unchained, and he began making preparations to go to Granada, where the royal court was now in residence, to appear before Ferdinand and Isabella.

Chapter 14

Setbacks and Frustration

When Christopher arrived at the royal court in Granada for an audience with the king and queen, his two sons, Diego and Ferdinand, hardly recognized him. Christopher understood why. In the time he had been away, he'd aged well beyond his forty-nine years. His hair was now completely gray, his face was deeply wrinkled, and he was suffering from arthritis and gout that made it painful for him to walk. Still, father and sons enjoyed a warm reunion as Christopher poured out to them the troubles that had befallen him.

Finally Christopher was led before the king and queen. But where he had been ebullient before their Highnesses during past audiences, this time he stood silent. Somehow the words would not come as he wanted. Instead he was overcome with the trials and tribulations he had undergone since his last audience. Wordlessly Christopher sank to his knees and wept uncontrollably. After several minutes of this, Isabella asked him to rise and speak.

Christopher staggered to his feet and began to pour out his tale of woe. He told the king and queen of the humiliation of being arrested and put in chains by Francisco de Bobadilla on Hispaniola, an island over which he had been made governor and viceroy by their Highnesses. He also listed other grievances that Bobadilla had inflicted upon him, including the confiscation of his gold, money, and other personal possessions and the possessions of his brothers. He pointed out that he had always been a loyal servant of the king and queen, and he demanded that they punish Bobadilla for his actions and that he, Christopher, be reinstated to his rightful position of governor and viceroy. He also asked that he be allowed to make a fourth voyage of discovery to the Indies.

Ferdinand and Isabella listened carefully to Christopher, but they did not respond to his requests immediately. They informed him that they needed time to contemplate all he had said.

Several months passed before Christopher was summoned to the royal court once again. But the response of Ferdinand and Isabella was not what Christopher had hoped for. The king and queen announced that they would allow him to retain the titles of governor and viceroy but that they would be titles only. Any power they conferred on him was stripped away. He would, however, be allowed to continue receiving the agreed-upon amount of income from trade with the islands he had discovered. And although they refused to punish Bobadilla for his actions on Hispaniola, since they had sent him as their representative, they had decided to recall him as governor of the island. In his stead, they told Christopher, they had appointed Nicolás de Ovando as the new governor of Hispaniola. Ovando would soon be setting sail for the island with a fleet of thirty-two ships and twenty-five hundred men to assume his new position. As a concession to Christopher, they agreed to allow him to send a representative to Hispaniola on Ovando's fleet with a royal mandate to retrieve and return to Spain all the goods and property taken from Christopher and his brothers at the time of their arrest. Much to Christopher's disappointment, the king and queen said nothing about another voyage to the Indies.

Christopher was confused and disappointed by the king and queen's decision. He had been so sure that they would act to fully vindicate him, but they had not. Now they were sending out another fleet to the Indies without him as a part of it. And although Ferdinand and Isabella had not said so, Christopher learned that at the royal court he was considered out of touch and irrelevant to the ongoing exploration of the Indies. Other explorers had voyaged north and south of the islands he had discovered, finding vast landmasses. Many geographers were now postulating that this was a huge and previously undiscovered continent. Also, these new explorers were proving to be more adept than Christopher in their exploration of the Indies—*his* Indies.

Christopher was aware of the discoveries of these new explorers and had even seen maps that now drew a large, unknown continent north, south, and west of the islands he had discovered. But he could not accept this proposition. These new explorers had sailed north and south of the Indies, but none of them had gone farther west. If they had, they would see he was right. After all, he had studied the writings of the ancient philosophers and geographers, and none of them said anything about a large, unknown continent. His own calculations of the circumference of the earth left only one possibility: the place where this new continent was said to lie was in the same place as the edge of the Asian continent. All that was needed was more exploration to the west and he would be proved right. Besides, hadn't God been guiding him to the riches and bounty of the East and to the Christian kingdom of Prester John? Surely God would not have led him to some other place, some other continent not yet explored or documented.

The more Christopher thought about it, the more he knew he needed to make one more trip to the Indies to prove to everyone that he was indeed right. If Colba (Cuba) was a peninsula of the mainland of Cathay (China), he reasoned, if he sailed westward to the end of the peninsula, he would reach the mainland of Asia proper. And if he followed that mainland south along what Marco Polo had called the Malay peninsula, he would come to the strait that Marco Polo had passed through into the Indian Ocean on his trip from Cathay to India. If Christopher found that strait, he could sail through it himself and head westward across the Indian Ocean around the bottom of Africa and back to Spain.

With this in mind he once again petitioned the king and queen for permission to undertake another voyage of exploration. But still their Highnesses would not approve such a voyage.

Christopher's heart sank when on February 13, 1502, Nicolás de Ovando and his fleet of ships set sail with great fanfare from Cádiz for Hispaniola. Christopher could not help but think that he should have been on the deck of the flagship, waving to the adoring crowds on the shore.

Once again Christopher petitioned Ferdinand and Isabella to be allowed to undertake another voyage of exploration to the Indies. To his surprise, a month after Ovando's departure, Christopher's petition was granted. The king and queen authorized the sending out of a second fleet under Christopher's leadership. But the contrast to Ovando's fleet could not have been more striking. Ovando had sailed with thirty-two ships and twenty-five hundred men in his fleet, while Christopher was allowed only four small caravels, all of which were overdue for extensive refitting. The four ships were the flagship *La Capitana*, under the command of Captain Diego Tristan, who had sailed with Christopher on his second voyage; *La Gallega*, captained by Pedro de Terreros, who had sailed with Christopher on all three of the previous voyages; the *Bermuda*, commanded by Francisco Porras; and the *Vizcaína*, under the command of a Genoese captain, Bartolomeo Fieschi. Christopher had confidence in all the captains except Porras, whom the king had ordered be included on the voyage along with Francisco's brother Diego. Francisco Porras had never captained a ship before, and his brother seemed critical of just about every order Christopher gave. Christopher worried that the two brothers would prove disloyal in an emergency, but since a high-ranking official had petitioned the king for them to be included on the voyage, Christopher could do little about it.

Instead of worrying about the Porras brothers, Christopher put his energy into gathering a crew. Because it was more difficult than ever to attract grown men to the endeavor, he ended up recruiting fifty-six boys under the age of fourteen as sailors. Among them was thirteen-year-old Ferdinand Columbus, who volunteered to sail with his father. Christopher was also able to convince his brother Bartholomew to sail with him again, despite the difficulties he had already endured in the Indies.

Young sailors made up most of the 140-man crew that sailed out of Cádiz harbor on May 9, 1502. Their mission was similar to the three previous voyages—find the mainland of Cathay. However, this time Christopher had been given strict instructions on where *not* to go. The king and queen warned him not to visit Hispaniola unless it was a matter of life or death. They did not want him stirring up trouble there.

Although Christopher was unhappy about not being able to return to Hispaniola, his hopes were set on discovering the strait that led from the Indies into the Indian Ocean. In case he found this strait and sailed around the world back to Spain, the king and queen had drafted a letter that he carried with him introducing him to the Portuguese explorer Vasco da Gama. Ferdinand and Isabella thought that the two explorers' fleets might meet each other somewhere in the middle of the Indian Ocean.

The four small caravels had steady winds on the outward passage. Despite the inexperienced crew, they crossed the Ocean Sea in twenty-one days, the fastest crossing Christopher had made on any of his trips. The small fleet made landfall on the island of Martinique, and everyone went ashore to bathe and wash their clothes in the freshwater streams of the island.

As they rested, Christopher looked northwestward toward Hispaniola. He wondered how Nicolás de Ovando was faring as the new governor of the island. And what ships lay at anchor in Santo Domingo harbor? The *Bermuda* had proved to be a hard vessel to handle on the crossing of the Ocean Sea, and Christopher contemplated going to Santo Domingo and trading her for a more agile vessel in which to continue his exploration. Besides, he told himself, he needed to send a letter back to the king and queen to let them know that the four caravels had made it safely to the Indies, and the only way to do that was to visit Hispaniola. Before long Christopher had convinced himself that he should head in that direction, and on June 29 he ordered anchors aweigh, and the ships set course for Hispaniola.

A day later Christopher was having serious doubts, not about his destination but about the weather. The sea had taken on an oily look, and his arthritic joints ached, sure signs of a coming storm. But how big would the storm be? Christopher had weathered two hurricanes in the Indies, and as he watched the waves and the clouds, he was sure that he was about to encounter his third hurricane. Now, he told himself, it really was a matter of life or death to get to the shelter of Hispaniola.

Just outside the harbor at Santo Domingo, Christopher had the ships heave to. He sent Pedro de Terreros, his senior captain, ashore to request permission to enter the harbor and seek shelter from the coming hurricane. He also sent a letter with Pedro to Nicolás de Ovando, warning him of the coming hurricane and advising him not to let any ships leave the harbor until the storm had passed.

When Pedro arrived back at the ship, Christopher could scarcely believe that Ovando had refused him permission to enter the harbor and seek shelter from the storm. Furthermore, Pedro reported, the governor had ridiculed the whole notion that Christopher could predict what the weather was going to be. He had even read aloud Christopher's letter of warning about the storm to his cronies in a derogatory manner as they laughed along uproariously. And if that were not enough, a fleet of thirty ships was departing that afternoon for Spain, and Ovando refused to delay their departure.

Stunned, Christopher set sail in search of shelter from the coming hurricane. He found the shelter he was looking for near the mouth of the Rio Jaina, a short distance west of Santo Domingo. Christopher ordered his captains to batten down their ships and double their anchor lines. He and his captains also came up with a contingency plan should the four ships be separated during the storm. If that happened, they were to sail to Puerto Viejo de Azua, fifty miles to the west.

Within hours, the winds had risen to gale force, mercilessly whipping up the surface of the sea and tossing the four caravels around like corks. As the hours passed, the intensity of the wind increased, as did the ferociousness of the ocean. The sky was leaden, lightning zigzagged above them, and rain pelted down. The crew were petrified of the storm, and Christopher tried to calm their fears. He had lost count of how many hours the storm had been lashing them when first the anchor cable of the *Bermuda* snapped, followed soon afterward by the anchor cables of *La Gallega* and the *Vizcaína*. The three caravels drifted apart and out to sea and soon disappeared from view into the murky grayness. Christopher ordered the crew of *La Capitana* to check the anchor lines and to do everything necessary to stop them from snapping. The crew were successful, and by the time the storm began to abate, the ship was still at anchor off the mouth of the Rio Jaina.

It was not long before Christopher and his crew noticed flotsam and jetsam floating on the surface of the ocean. Christopher feared the worst, and those fears were confirmed with the arrival of a messenger from Santo Domingo. The hurricane had struck the fleet of ships on their way to Spain as they sailed through the Mona Passage at the eastern end of Hispaniola. The result was disastrous. Nineteen of the ships had been sunk, with all hands aboard lost. Six other ships had also sunk, but there were a few survivors from them. Four more ships had managed to limp back to Santo Domingo badly damaged and barely afloat, and one ship, the *Aguja*, had made it through the storm and was continuing on to Spain. Christopher learned that Alonso Sánchez Carvajal was aboard this vessel. Carvajal was the agent Christopher had dispatched to Hispaniola to retrieve the gold and other possessions confiscated from him and his brothers by Francisco de Bobadilla. The gold and possessions were being transported to Spain on the *Aguja*.

Christopher breathed a sigh of relief. Then he learned another piece of stunning news. All of the other gold collected on Hispaniola had been loaded aboard the flagship of the returning fleet and had gone to the bottom of the ocean along with the stricken ship. Also traveling aboard the flagship were the two men who had caused so much trouble for him and his brothers on Hispaniola, Francisco de Bobadilla and Francisco Roldán. Both men had drowned when the ship sank during the hurricane.

Despite the tragedy, Christopher felt a sense of justice in it. *His* gold was on its way safely to Spain, while his tormentors and *their* gold lay lost on the floor of the ocean. Nonetheless, Christopher was bitter toward Ovando for not allowing him to take shelter in the harbor at Santo Domingo. In a letter to Ferdinand and Isabella he complained of Ovando's decision, saying, "What man ever born, not excepting Job, would not have died of despair when in such weather, seeking safety for son, brother, shipmates and myself, we were forbidden the land and the harbor that I, by God's will and sweating blood, won for Spain!"

After finishing his letter to their Highnesses, Christopher set sail in *La Capitana* westward to Puerto Viejo de Azua, where he hoped to learn the fate of the other three ships in his fleet. His heart sank when *La Capitana* sailed into the small harbor on Sunday, July 3, and the other three ships were not there. But Christopher's spirits were lifted when, over the next several hours, the three ships arrived in the harbor with spine-tingling stories to tell of riding out the hurricane.

The four caravels stayed at anchor in Puerto Viejo de Azua for a week, making preparations for the next leg of their journey. Then they set sail west, passing the south coasts of Jamesque (Jamaica) and Colba and setting out across the sea. On July 13, 1502, after three days of sailing, they reached an island. The ships anchored off the island, and Bartholomew Columbus took a party of men ashore. When he returned, he explained to Christopher that the inhabitants of the island had a much more advanced civilization than the natives on the other side of the sea. These people were weavers and metalworkers who worked with copper tools. They did not go naked but dressed in woven tunics and robes dyed bright colors. And the men were armed with battle-axes and flint-edged swords. They traveled about in huge dugout canoes, many with enclosed cabins on them.

Christopher was delighted with what he was hearing. These were more like the people he had expected to find in the Indies. It could only mean he was right: they were close to the mainland of Asia.

Sure enough, the ships sailed on and soon reached the coast of a vast mainland. Gleefully Christopher gave the order for the ships to follow the coastline in a southerly direction. Soon he would be proved right. It would not be long now before he found the strait that led to the Indian Ocean.

As the four caravels began to follow the coastline, they were engulfed in a huge storm. For the next twenty-eight days, strong head winds, rough seas, and torrential rain buffeted the ships. To make matters worse, along this part of the coast there were no harbors in which to take shelter at night. Instead the ships were forced to anchor in the open sea, tugging at their anchorlines as they pitched and rolled in the swell, making life aboard extremely uncomfortable for everyone.

It was not long before the crew began to despair of surviving the voyage. They started to pray and make vows to go on pilgrimages if God helped them make it through the storm. Still the storm persisted, and the crew begged Christopher to turn back and head for Hispaniola. But Christopher felt he had come too far to turn back now, and so the fleet pushed on. Progress against the storm, though, was slow, and in the twenty-eight days they were caught in its grip, they covered only 170 miles.

The storm took its toll on Christopher's health. The constant buffeting of the ship aggravated his arthritis and gout, and the deep scars on his wrists and ankles from the fetters while he was under arrest opened up and began to bleed. Sometimes they bled so profusely that Christopher feared that he would die. He did not die, but he became so weak that the crew built him a small, doghouse-like structure on the poop deck in which he could sit, see what was going on, and call out orders.

On one occasion during the storm a huge waterspout was spotted heading toward the ships. The crew stood petrified. Most of them had never seen such a phenomenon. While they stood staring, Christopher scrambled to his feet, found his Bible, and read aloud from it the account of Jesus' walking on the water. When he had finished reading, he rebuked the storm, pulled out his sword, and slashed a cross in the air. Much to everyone's amazement, the waterspout bypassed the ships.

Finally, on September 14, the ships reached a point where the coastline turned more directly south. As they rounded the point, Christopher named it Cape Gracias a Dios (Thanks Be to God). Once around the cape they were sailing almost directly south and were no longer battling a stiff head wind and the current.

As they made their way south, the ships made periodic stops, often near the mouths of rivers, where groups of sailors went ashore to explore. The sailors returned with reports of seeing pumas, deer, monkeys, and crocodiles. They also reported that the Indians here were different from those clad in bright tunics on the island they had encountered. These Indians were more like those on Hispaniola. They painted their faces red and black, and they bored holes in their ears.

At one of these stops, as the caravels were anchored off a river mouth, Christopher sent a boat ashore to replenish the fresh water supply. As the boat was crossing the bar in the river mouth, a wave swamped it, and two of the men aboard were drowned. Christopher named the river Rio de los Desastres (River of Disasters).

At each stop, using gestures and sign language, Christopher quizzed the natives as to whether they knew about the strait he was looking for, and on one occasion he was told of a narrow strait that led to a vast sea. Excitedly Christopher sailed on, following the directions the Indians had given him. He found the narrow strait; it was just big enough for the ships to squeeze through. Alas, it led not to the Indian Ocean but to a large, inland saltwater lagoon. Disappointed, Christopher continued his exploration along the coast.

Soon after encountering the lagoon, the explorers came to an area the natives said was called Veragua. In this region the Indians adorned their chests with gold disks, and some also wore gold bird-shaped amulets around their necks. They willingly traded the gold disks and amulets with the Spaniards for two hawk's bells apiece, worth one penny. The Indians also informed Christopher that the gold items they wore were made from gold nuggets that they dug from the side of the hills, using their knives.

Christopher duly noted this in his log as a reminder to come back and explore this region further. For now his mission was to find the elusive strait that led to the Indian Ocean. He was surprised that he had not yet discovered it. The Malay peninsula was proving to be longer than he had thought. But as he sailed farther along the coast, his hope of finding the strait was dashed. The Indians informed him that the land he was sailing along was a narrow isthmus, and there was no river or strait that bisected it so that a ship could sail from the ocean on one side to the ocean on the other side.

With this information Christopher disappointedly decided to turn back and further explore the Veragua region. The four caravels retraced their path along the coast as Christopher searched for a suitable site to establish a trading post. He found the site in the mouth of a river he named Rio Belén (Bethlehem). Just enough water was flowing over the bar in the river mouth for the four caravels to cross it, and on January 6, 1503, the ships dropped anchor in the small basin behind the bar.

At first the Indians in the area were friendly toward the Spaniards, providing them with food and, of course, gold. But Christopher noticed a change in their attitude as they watched the trading post being built, until they became openly hostile toward the Spaniards.

As work on building the trading post drew to a close, the water level in the river began to drop. Three of the caravels, *La Capitana*, *Bermuda*, and *Vizcaína*, had to be hauled over the bar and back to sea lest the water get so low that they became completely grounded. *La Gallega* was left in the basin, where it had been at anchor for three months. This vessel was to stay behind as a floating fortress for those staying to man the new trading post, which Christopher had named Santa María de Belén.

Christopher's plan was to leave his brother Bartholomew and twenty men behind to man Santa María de Belén. Christopher would then sail to Hispaniola to carry out some much-needed repairs on the ships and to load up with provisions to bring back to the trading post. The Indians had made several small attacks on the Spaniards and their new trading post. To ensure that they didn't attack while he was away, Christopher ordered his men to go ashore and capture thirty Indian hostages that he would take with him to Hispaniola. If the local

Indians were helpful while he was gone, the hostages would be released upon his return. The hostages were loaded into the hold of *La Capitana*. The following day, as the sailors said good-bye to those staying behind, the Indians attacked, killing several of the Spaniards and wounding Bartholomew. Christopher ordered the remainder of his crew ashore to help with the fight, but the Spaniards were greatly outnumbered.

With the sailors gone ashore, the Indian hostages in the hold decided they would rather die than be taken away by the Spanish, so they hanged themselves. When Christopher learned that the hostages were all dead, he realized he was in an impossible position. With no hostages and his men outnumbered in the fight, the only option was retreat. Christopher comforted himself with the idea that at a later date he could return with more men and retake the trading post. A volunteer swam ashore from *La Capitana* and delivered the order to abandon Santa María de Belén and *La Gallega* and retreat to the other ships. The men ashore hastily built a raft and began transferring to the three caravels. When all of them were aboard, Christopher gave the order for the ships to weigh anchor and sail away.

Christopher knew that he had to get to Hispaniola as fast as he could. His ships were in bad shape. Teredos, or shipworms, mollusks that bore into the wooden planking of a ship's hull, had attached themselves to the hulls of the three caravels. They had burrowed so far into the wooden hulls that the ships leaked badly, and no amount of bailing could keep up with the rate the water seeped in. It soon became obvious that *Vizcaína* was not going to make it. Her hull was too badly worm eaten, and she was sinking fast. Christopher ordered the vessel abandoned and her crew spread evenly between *La Capitana* and *Bermuda*. The two vessels then made a dash north for Santo Domingo. However, Christopher had misjudged their position. He had assumed that they were on the same meridian as Hispaniola as they headed north. But when they reached the shores of Colba instead, Christopher knew that he was in trouble. He turned east and tried to make a run for Santo Domingo. But the ships were sinking too fast, and he knew that they would not make it. He had to act fast, so he gave the order for the two leaking caravels to change course to the south toward Jamesque.

Christopher was immensely relieved when both vessels sailed into Santa Gloria Bay on the north coast of Jamesque. The ships were incapable of sailing any farther, and Christopher ordered *La Capitana* and the *Bermuda* to be beached side by side. They were safe. But they were also now marooned on Jamesque, and not one person in the outside world knew where they were.

Chapter 15

Home Again

Christopher ordered that the ships be shored up with timbers so that they would stand upright on an even keel on the beach. Palm-thatched cabins were constructed on their decks, and the two stricken hulks served as both home and fortress for the marooned sailors. A large, friendly Indian village was situated nearby, but Christopher fretted that the Indians might not stay so friendly if his men mixed with them and the usual misunderstandings arose. As a result, he gave strict orders for his men to stay on the ships or on the beach beside them and not to go anywhere near the village. Instead, he sent Diego Méndez, who had proved to be one of the most able men on the voyage, to negotiate with the Indians.

It was not long before Diego had worked out a system whereby the Indians would supply the

Spaniards with food. In return the Indians would receive two glass beads for every loaf of cassava bread they supplied; two lace points for two hutia, the large rodents Christopher's crew had eaten on Colba during his second voyage; and two hawk's bells for any large quantity of fish, maize, or other items they supplied. The system worked well. The Indians were happy with the items they received in payment, and the crew were not starving.

With the food supply solved, Christopher turned his attention to getting off Jamesque (Jamaica). The two caravels were beyond repair, and Christopher and his men did not have the necessary tools to cut timber and build a new vessel. They waited in the hope that some ship might pass by the north coast of Jamesque and spot the ships aground on the beach. After four months of waiting, this seemed unlikely, and another plan of action was called for. Finally it was decided that Diego Méndez and the Genoan, Bartolomeo Fieschi, would take two canoes and try to make it to Hispaniola and then on to Santo Domingo to get help.

Each man took with him six Spaniards and ten Indians to paddle the canoes. As the two canoes set out, Christopher hoped and prayed they would be successful. It was 108 miles from their position on Jamesque to the southwestern tip of Hispaniola, and then another 250 miles along the island's south coast to reach Santo Domingo. The chances of the two canoes not making it were great, but it was a gamble Christopher knew they had to take.

After six months marooned on Jamesque and no way of knowing whether Diego and Bartolomeo had made it to Santo Domingo, Christopher was aware that his men were beginning to despair. He did his best to keep their spirits up, but he had to admit to himself that it was a halfhearted attempt, because he himself was having doubts about ever getting off Jamesque. His health was poor, he was suffering from malaria, and he began to think that this island might be his final resting place. Little did Christopher know that Francisco and Diego Porras were stirring up a mutiny against him. The Porras brothers secretly secured the support of forty-six of the men. Christopher suddenly became aware of the mutiny on New Year's Day 1504, when under the cry "To Castile! To Castile!" the rebels stormed off the two stricken ships, stole ten Indian dugout canoes, captured a number of Indians to paddle them, and set off eastward along the coast. As they went, Christopher soon learned, they had plundered other Indian villages before heading out to sea, hoping to make it to Hispaniola in their canoes.

Later Christopher learned even more about the plight of the mutineers. The men had gone about fifteen miles out to sea when a strong wind began to blow, forcing them to head back to shore. As they went, in a frantic attempt to stay afloat in the roughening sea, they dumped their plunder from the Indian villages overboard, along with the Indians they had abducted to paddle the canoes. They made two more attempts to get to Hispaniola, and both times they were forced back to Jamesque by unfavorable weather conditions. Eventually they gave up their plan and trudged back to Santa Gloria

Bay and set up camp in the jungle near the beach, where Christopher had his men then keep a careful eye on them lest they create more havoc.

By now another problem was plaguing Christopher. The Indians had grown tired of supplying the Spaniards with food. They now had more glass beads, hawk's bells, and lace points than they knew what to do with. They also complained that one Spaniard ate as much food as ten or twenty Indians, a fact Christopher had already noted himself. As a result, the supply of food from the Indians had dwindled to virtually nothing, and the men were going hungry. Christopher was surprised that even gnawing hunger did not motivate his crew to do anything about it. There was an abundance of fish in the bay, but none of the men tried to catch any to supplement their diet. Instead they looked to Christopher to solve their problem.

Finally Christopher thought he had just the plan to convince the Indians to start supplying them again with food. He had with him an almanac that predicted a total eclipse of the moon on the last night of February 1504. On that day Christopher called together the cacique and other leaders of the village for a meeting. At the meeting he told the natives that God desired them to provide the Spaniards food, and God was not pleased with them that they were no longer doing so. As a result, God was going to send them a sign of his displeasure in the sky that very evening. When the moon came out, Christopher told them, they should watch it very closely.

Sure enough, as the almanac had predicted, that evening as the moon rose above the horizon, it began to be eclipsed. It was not long before the terrified cacique and his headmen from the village came running to the ship, calling out for Christopher. They begged him to pray to his God to make the moon bright again. If he did, they promised that they would continue to supply the Spaniards with food. Christopher retired to his cabin, as if to pray, and came again when he knew the moon was about to emerge from the eclipse. He told the natives that God had taken them at their word. And because they had promised to keep supplying food, He would make the moon shine again for them. With that the moon began to emerge and light up the night sky. The Indians were terrified and awestruck by what had happened, and the supply of food to Christopher and his men started again immediately.

By the end of March 1504, more than nine months had passed since Christopher and his men had been marooned on Jamesque. Still the men did not know whether Diego and Bartolomeo had made it to Santo Domingo. Then suddenly one day a caravel appeared in Santa Gloria Bay and dropped anchor. It was the first ship other than those in their own fleet that the men had seen in nearly two years. Excitement ran high as a boat rowed ashore. Their rescue was at hand!

The men's excitement soon faded when the men learned that Nicolás de Ovando had sent the ship not to rescue them but to check up on what Christopher was up to. However, the captain of the ship, Diego de Escobar, informed them that Diego Méndez and Bartolomeo Fieschi had made it to Hispaniola alive and that Diego had gone on to Santo Domingo, where he was trying to charter a vessel to sail to Jamesque to rescue them. The captain also delivered a gift from Ovando, a side of salt pork and other food from Spain. Having determined that Christopher and his men were still alive, the caravel sailed away, much to the chagrin of those left marooned on the island. Christopher, for his part, was incensed. It was yet another insult and humiliation that he had to bear at the hands of his opponent.

Despite his injured pride, Christopher, like the rest of his crew, held on to the hope that they would soon be rescued. Diego Méndez had proved himself over and over again as a man of action. And if he was trying to charter a ship to rescue them, that is what he would surely do.

As Christopher thought about being rescued and finally making it back to Spain, he also thought about the Porras brothers. The brothers had been royal appointees to the expedition, and if he was going to make it back to Spain, he had better make sure that these rebellious brothers made it back safely as well. Since he did not want to have to explain to Ferdinand and Isabella why he had left them behind on Jamesque, he decided to try and reconcile with the brothers.

Christopher sent a representative to arrange a meeting with Francisco and Diego Porras, but the meeting did not go well. The two brothers made excessive demands of Christopher that he refused to meet. Rather than making peace, the meeting seemed to stir up old animosities between the brothers and Christopher. This resulted in their attacking and trying to overrun the two ships on May 19. As a result, a battle followed. Bartholomew Columbus rallied the crew still loyal to Christopher, and they pursued the Porras brothers and their band of mutineers. They engaged them in a fierce sword fight in which a number of men were killed. From the deck of the beached *La Capitana*, Christopher watched as his brother finally got the upper hand and the mutineers surrendered.

After the battle Christopher pardoned all of the mutineers except the Porras brothers, whom he had chained.

On June 29, 1504, one year and five days after being marooned on Jamesque, Christopher was jubilant. A caravel with Diego Méndez aboard sailed into Santa Gloria Bay. Their rescue really was at hand this time. The men let out a loud cheer as the vessel dropped anchor. Twenty-four hours later Christopher and his marooned men were on their way to Santo Domingo.

When Christopher finally set foot again on Hispaniola, it was almost too much to take in. Jamesque was not going to be his grave after all. But conditions on Hispaniola under Ovando's leadership were worse than ever, and Christopher was glad on September 12 to board a chartered caravel bound for Spain.

Sailing on the caravel with Christopher were his son Ferdinand, his brother Bartholomew, and twenty-two other members of the original crew. The remainder of the crew had been unwilling to face another sea voyage and had decided to stay behind on Hispaniola. As the voyage across the Ocean Sea dragged on, Christopher began to wonder whether those members of his crew might have made the smarter decision by staying behind. The ship got caught up in a severe storm in which its mainmast snapped. Christopher and Bartholomew had to rig a jury mast, using a spare yardarm. Finally, on November 7, 1504, fifty-six days after setting out from Santo Domingo, the ship made its arrival in Cádiz.

By the time Christopher stepped ashore in Cádiz, he was a tired and sick man. His arthritis and gout were so painful that he could barely walk, and he was still feverish and weak from malaria. He had to be escorted to Seville, where he moved into a rented house. Meanwhile, Christopher's now sixteen-year-old son, Ferdinand, returned to his position in the royal court, full of tales of hardship and adventure across the Ocean Sea. At the royal court he was reunited with twenty-five-year-old Diego Columbus, who was now a well-liked and respected member of the royal guard.

Christopher expected that it would not be long before he, too, was back at the royal court for an audience with their Highnesses. But no official invitation for an audience with the king and queen was forthcoming. Christopher soon learned why: Queen Isabella was ill and confined to bed. Christopher hoped that after she was better, she would invite him for an audience with her and the king. But this was not to be. On November 26, 1504, Isabella died. Christopher was grief-stricken when he heard the news. He thought that she, more than anyone else in the world, understood him, and now she was gone. He desperately wanted to attend her funeral, but he had to face the fact that he was not well enough to travel. In fact, the queen's death reminded him of his own mortality. Isabella had been the same age as he.

After the queen's death, Christopher focused his attention on two matters. First, he believed that the Crown was not giving him the full amount due him from trade with the lands he had discovered, an amount that was guaranteed in the *Capitulations* he and the king and queen had agreed to in 1492. Second, the Crown was refusing to pay the wages due the crew who had made the fourth voyage with him. The royal court had taken the position that the men were due nothing for the year they spent marooned on Jamesque because, in effect, they were not working during that time. Most of those who had sailed on the voyage with Christopher had been poor, and now with no wages for the two and a half years they had been away, many of them were desperate.

Christopher made repeated submissions to the royal court to deal with these issues but made no progress. Then, in early May 1505, Christopher received some good news. He had been summoned for an audience before King Ferdinand to discuss the issues. He set out immediately for Segovia, three hundred miles away, where the royal court was presently seated. Christopher rode on the back of a mule, because his arthritis made it too painful for him to ride on a horse.

As he was led before the king, Christopher had high hopes that both issues would soon be settled. But he left disappointed. Ferdinand was not as kindly disposed toward Christopher as his wife had been. He suggested that an arbitrator decide the matter of how much Christopher should receive from trade with the Indies. Christopher refused this suggestion, pointing out that there was no need for an arbitrator because the *Capitulations* was a clear and binding agreement between him and the Crown that needed to be honored, not arbitrated. On the matter of back pay for the members of his crew, the king refused this request, stating once again that the men did not deserve to be paid for the year they were marooned.

Christopher left the royal court bitter and disheartened at Ferdinand's unwillingness to hear him. He made his way to Valladolid, sixty miles away, where he felt the climate was better, and rented a room for the next year. Eventually, Christopher could feel his strength fading away, and he set about writing a new draft of his will. In the document he designated Diego the heir to all his titles and positions and instructed him to provide from his estate for the other family members. He also instructed that part of his fortune be deposited in San Giorgio Bank in Genoa to be used at some future date to finance a crusade to liberate Jerusalem.

On May 19, 1506, so weak that he was barely able to move, Christopher had the will ratified and took to his bed. The following day his condition grew worse. Christopher's sons, Diego and Ferdinand, were at his side, as were his brothers Bartholomew and Diego, along with Diego Méndez and Bartolomeo Fieschi, who had served him faithfully throughout the fourth voyage. When they saw Christopher's condition worsening, they sent for the local priest, who said Mass and administered the sacraments. After a final prayer, Christopher roused himself to utter his final words. In Latin he repeated the last words of Jesus Christ on the cross: "In manus tuas, Domine, commendo spiritum meum [Into Thy hands, O Lord, I commit my spirit]." A few moments later Christopher Columbus died. The date was May 20, 1506, and Christopher was fifty-four years old.

The funeral that followed was a simple affair, more fit for a peasant than that of the Admiral of the Ocean Sea and the Governor and Viceroy of the Islands and Lands of the Indies. It was the local village priest and not a bishop who said the Mass, and no dignitaries or royal representatives were present.

Despite the lack of public recognition at his funeral, no one could deny Christopher's accomplishments. While he may have died in obscurity, the magnitude of his discoveries across the Ocean Sea was just beginning to be realized. The great irony of it all was that Christopher Columbus never himself realized the magnitude of his discoveries. Christopher died believing that he had made it to the Asian mainland, never realizing that the land he had stood upon was a vast continent that would soon be known as America.

Bibliography

De Hevesy, André. *The Discoverers: A New Narrative of the Life and Hazardous Adventures of the Genoese Christopher Columbus.* The Macaulay Company, 1928.

Dodge, Stephen C. *Christopher Columbus and the First Voyages to the New World.* New York: Chelsea House Publishers, 1991.

Dolan, Sean J. *Christopher Columbus: The Intrepid Mariner.* New York: Fawcett Columbine, 1989.

Fernández-Armesto, Felipe. *Columbus and the Conquest of the Impossible.* New York: Saturday Review Press, 1974.

Levinson, Nancy Smiler. *Christopher Columbus: Voyager to the Unknown.* New York: Lodestar Books, 1990.

Meltzer, Milton. *Columbus and the World around Him.* New York: Franklin Watts, 1990.

Meredith, Robert, and E. Brooks Smith, eds. *The Quest of Columbus.* Boston: Little, Brown and Company, 1966.

Morison, Samuel Eliot. *Christopher Columbus: Mariner.* Penguin Group, 1942.

Soule, Gardner. *Christopher Columbus: On the Green Sea of Darkness.* New York: Franklin Watts, 1988.